Praise for
The Very Good Gospel

"Lisa Sharon Harper has presented the gospel, the good news, as it was meant to be—whole and complete. Our world has compromised so many elements of the good news that we are left with a divided gospel. We need to recover the whole Christian gospel, the wholeness of the church, the wholeness of relationships. Lisa has unleashed the whole-ism of shalom. Her application of the good news for America, for our culture, in the world, reminds us that God is bigger than our problems. My wish is that Christians and non-Christians alike read this book."

—DR. JOHN PERKINS, co-founder of the Christian Community
Development Association, founder of the John and Vera
Mac Perkins Foundation in Jackson, Mississippi, and author
of *Let Justice Roll Down*

"Lisa Sharon Harper is so smart and interesting—she's a wonderful leader. I respect her immensely and am passionate about the message of this book."

—JEN HATMAKER, speaker and best-selling author of *For the Love*

"For anyone who has ever wondered if we were meant for more, Lisa Sharon Harper's *The Very Good Gospel* provides a resounding yes, revealing God's eternal vision of shalom for all creation—people, families, genders, races, and the nations. Our gospel has long been presented in a shallow way—and unattractive in its narrowness. *The Very Good Gospel* declares the breadth of God's Word, reconciling social justice and personal salvation, and inviting readers to share the rich message of shalom for all people, as it was intended."

—MICHAEL ERIC DYSON, political analyst, professor, and best-
selling author of *The Black Presidency: Barack Obama and
the Politics of Race in America*

"For many decades, both mainline Christianity and the evangelical church have been captive to competing, shallow, and 'thin' understandings of what the good news of the gospel really is. In *The Very Good Gospel*, Lisa Sharon Harper masterfully presents the case that the very good news God brings to us is about the restoration of shalom—that is to say peace, well-being, wholeness, and abundance—which conquers the false dichotomy between social justice and personal salvation. Lisa shows us that God's creation is emphatically, even forcefully, *good,* and it is the duty of *every* human being to responsibly steward God's creation. Lisa's clear, evocative prose blends scholarly theological insights with moving life experiences to show the clear applications of the gospel to our cross-gender relationships, our struggle against racism, how we care for the environment, our relationships with ourselves, and much more. I strongly recommend this book to anyone who seeks to understand God's true purpose for the world and for our lives."

— JIM WALLIS, *New York Times* best-selling author of *America's Original Sin: Racism, White Privilege, and the Bridge to a New America,* president of Sojourners, and editor-in-chief of *Sojourners* magazine

"There are lots of 'gospels' out there competing for our affection—the gospel of the Kardashians, of Trump, of American exceptionalism—but Lisa Sharon Harper dives into the one true gospel, God's very good news. On these pages, the Garden of Eden meets the world we live in. Harper stirs up an ancient, radical vision of shalom, whereby God heals all the wounds that sin has created—in our hearts, in our streets, and in our world."

—SHANE CLAIBORNE, activist and author of *Executing Grace*

"To speak of the gospel as good news, it has to be good news for the oppressed, the impoverished, the brokenhearted. To embody God's shalom is to embrace and restore the image of God in all humanity no matter who or where they are. Chapter by chapter Lisa Sharon Harper builds the case for reading, understanding, and living the gospel as the life-giving, freedom-bringing, shalom-infused reality it really is. There are new, exciting voices coming from a new, younger generation of evangelicals, and they are turning the traditional meaning of that word around. Lisa Sharon Harper is such a voice and well worth hearing."

—ALLAN BOESAK, South African human-rights activist
    and the Desmond Tutu Chair of Peace, Justice, and
    Reconciliation Studies at Christian Theological Seminary
    and Butler University

"Lisa Sharon Harper writes in a fresh and personal way, combining rich theology with deep experience working with contemporary issues to inspire us not to settle for a thin gospel but a thick gospel—the fullness of the good news of God's reconciliation and shalom that touches all aspects of life. *The Very Good Gospel* is for all of us struggling with how the good news of Jesus should impact not just our own lives but also speak to the injustices in our world. This book brings all the threads together and weaves a glorious picture of God's redemptive work in creation."

—KEN WYTSMA, president of Kilns College and author
    of *Pursuing Justice* and *Create vs. Copy*

"Exposing racism, sexism, and exploitation as a direct assault on God, *The Very Good Gospel* weaves its wisdom around God's shalom—the blessed web of creation, where the flourishing of one is a flourishing of all. It is beautiful and true. Thank you, Lisa!"

—DR. MIMI HADDAD, president of Christians for Biblical
    Equality, www.cbeinternational.org

"Part mountaineer, part miner, Lisa Sharon Harper has somehow ascended the mountain of Scripture to survey its entirety while also digging deep into its core to extract raw truth of immense implication and conviction. Lisa's revealing stories, scriptural depth, and prophetic voice make *The Very Good Gospel* a very good read—one you won't want to miss."

—DAVID DRURY, chief of staff for the Wesleyan Church World
  Headquarters and author of nine books including *Transforming
  Presence*

"One can scan across the landscape of the church and not find a better articulator of the essence of the gospel in the twenty-first century. Lisa Sharon Harper follows a rich tradition of reformers and iconoclast theological practitioners who deeply love the gospel and God's people. She has made it her life's project to challenge lethargic and cynical people to live love and practice justice. Our world is richer and more vibrant because of her compassionate and strong voice."

—REVEREND DR. OTIS MOSS III, senior pastor of Trinity United
  Church of Christ and author of *Blue Note Preaching in a
  Post-Soul World*

"In a world that has legitimate reasons to question the possibility of a good God, Lisa Sharon Harper reminds us what is in fact not only good but beautiful about the God who loves us more than we want to be loved. Her winsome words wash over the reader with gentleness, while simultaneously striking out with a fierce love that is corrective and healing. *The Very Good Gospel* is more than just a social activist's field guide; it is a road map to a better world—one marked by faith, hope, and love."

—CHRISTOPHER L. HEUERTZ, author, activist, and founding
  partner of Gravity: A Center for Contemplative Activism

The Very Good Gospel

The VERY GOOD GOSPEL

How Everything Wrong Can Be Made Right

LISA SHARON HARPER

FOREWORD BY WALTER BRUEGGEMANN

WATERBROOK

Library of Congress Cataloging-in-Publication Data
Names: Harper, Lisa Sharon, author.
Title: The very good gospel : how everything wrong can be made right / foreword by Walter Brueggemann ; Lisa Sharon Harper.
Description: Colorado Springs, Colorado : WaterBrook Press, 2016. | Includes bibliographical references.
Identifiers: LCCN 2016002917 (print) | LCCN 2016012952 (ebook) | ISBN 9781601428578 (hardcover) | ISBN 9781601428592 (electronic)
Subjects: LCSH: Christianity—Essence, genius, nature. | Shalom (The Hebrew word) | Peace—Religious aspects—Christianity.
Classification: LCC BT60 .H376 2016 (print) | LCC BT60 (ebook) | DDC 230—dc23 LC record available at http://lccn.loc.gov/2016002917

Printed in the United States of America
2016—First Edition

10 9 8 7 6 5 4 3 2 1

For all those who long for more.

CONTENTS

FOREWORD

Lisa Sharon Harper has written a bracing, generative exposition of the elemental narrative of gospel faith. She has done so by sharing the sequence of the "very good" of creation, "the wreckage of the Fall," and the "very good" of the gospel of reconciliation and restoration.

The powerful witness of her book is an antidote to a "thin" reading of the gospel. By *thin* Harper means a surface reading that settles simply and immediately for what meets the eye and assumes that a quick summary gets it all. Such a reading of the gospel risks reducing it to a package of certitudes without recognition of the depth and mystery of the news. She examines the convenient fundamentalism that has too often given credence to racism and gender violence, and she addresses the progressive church and the flaws of "thin" theology.

Thus, Harper proposes a "thick" reading of the gospel. The notion of "thick description" has an important pedigree that's well worth noting. The phrase was first coined by Gilbert Ryle in his philosophic understanding of the world that refused simple scientific explanatory positivism. The term was taken up by Clifford Geertz in his cultural anthropology. Geertz insisted that conventional social-scientific observation could not possibly grasp—let alone explain—the significance of social symbols and practices in cultures other than our own. George Lindbeck used the term in his resistance to "propositional" or "expressive" theological method as he advocated a "cultural linguistic" approach.

In her book, Harper takes up the awareness of Ryle, Geertz, and Lindbeck and applies it to our discernment of the gospel. There is more to the gospel than meets the eye, so evangelical thought must be patient in its recognition of the inscrutable mystery of the God of the gospel who gives gifts and summons to tasks that do not fit our preconceived categories.

The capacity that Harper exhibits to move from thin to thick in her exposition of the gospel is empowered by her personal witness of faith and life. She knows firsthand about the racism and gender violence that arise from a thin rendering of the gospel. Indeed, she knows in her own life about the "wreckage of the Fall," whereby violence is inflected on one's neighbors. It took my breath away when I read of her third great-grandmother who was the last adult slave in her family on a plantation in South Carolina. One cannot overestimate the force of the memory and experience of such violence as a context for rereading the gospel.

Her melding of textually informed theology and her experience of violence result in a book that is compellingly thick. Harper addresses the deep wound-producing practices of our society and articulates the costly hope of healing inherent in the gospel. With acute insight, she details the interface between gospel faith and lived reality. *The Very Good Gospel* is a welcome read that invites a rethinking of faith and life that is all too often dumbed down to thin. Thinning our bodies may be good for our physical health, but such thinning of faith is a recipe for chaos and death. Harper bears witness to the thicker, truer understanding of a saving, transformative, reconciling faith that is indeed "very good."

Walter Brueggemann
Columbia Theological Seminary
October 12, 2015

The Very Good Gospel

There must be more to the gospel, I thought.

The gospel. Those words are weighed down with images of Bible-thumping television preachers, white robes, tambourines, street evangelists damning passersby to hell, and lace-collared door-knockers intent on spreading what they call the gospel. The Greek word translated as "gospel" in the Bible is *euangelion,* meaning "good message." Today we commonly translate it as "good news."

When we think of good news, we usually think about something that excites folks. News that makes people want to celebrate. I think of a Facebook post from a good friend who announced that she just got a job. Or the good news that a grant was approved. Or the good news that a nephew was accepted to all three of his top-pick colleges. Woo-hoo! It makes us want to shout, to celebrate. Someone pop the bubbly and turn up the music!

Christians are taught to think of the good news of Jesus Christ in this way:

God loves us, but we're sinful. As a result, we're separated from God. Jesus died to pay the penalty for our sins. All we have to do is believe that his death was enough and we get to go to heaven.

That's some good news. Seriously, who wants to languish in hell forever?

But on this particular day, as I walked away from the King Center in Atlanta, one thought haunted me: *The good news of my gospel doesn't feel good enough.*

It was the last stop on a pilgrimage taken by select staff from a national college ministry. At the time, I served as the ministry's director of racial reconciliation in Greater Los Angeles. Over four weeks, the pilgrimage took this diverse group of twenty-five key staff leaders and family members through ten states. We investigated two of the most brutal realities of US history: the Cherokee Trail of Tears and the experiences of Africans on American soil, from antebellum slavery to the civil rights movement of the 1960s.

I had been to the King Center just a few months before, so when we arrived on the last day of the pilgrimage, I planned to just mill around while the other group members got their fill. I wandered into the main hall. It all looked like it had when I'd seen it previously until I caught a glimpse of something unfamiliar. Paintings lined the walls. Between each painting a dollar bill was mounted. I was intrigued, so I moved closer. Here was a painting of enslaved people, and in the art they were happy.

What?

I found a plaque on the wall that offered instructions for how to move through the exhibit. It asked the viewer to examine the painting, then try to find that same picture on the dollar bill displayed next to it. I looked closely at the next painting. It was a different scene showing a different enslaved person. This man was carrying a beautiful basket full of cotton, and he was happy. And he had shoes. *How strange.* Most slaves didn't have shoes.

I could hear the line from an old spiritual born from the misery of plantation life. It declares, "All o' God's chillun got shoes."[1]

For an enslaved person, the differences between being a slave and being a white person were obvious. Whites had freedom of movement and thought, a declaration of their independence, and a Constitution that affirmed their equality. And in addition to *all of that*, white folk had shoes. Owning shoes represented human dignity. The saying "All o' God's chillun got shoes" seemed harmless to outsiders, but it was a statement of resistance. Having shoes served as a reminder to each member of the enslaved community that you are a child of God. Though the slave master and society do not recognize it, you were born with human dignity. There is a place in God's Kingdom where you have shoes!

So this painting of a happy slave carrying a beautiful basket of cotton while wearing neatly tied shoes struck me as odd. I followed the instructions of the exhibit and found the painting represented on the dollar bill mounted next to it. I moved to the next painting and viewed a scene of an idyllic countryside bursting with cotton. A straight-backed slave family—mother, father, and two children—picked cotton together. They were fully garbed with aprons to protect their clothing, and they all wore shoes.

I examined the dollar bill next to this painting. There was the same happy slave family in the lower-right corner of a ten-dollar note from Charleston, South Carolina. I searched for more information about the exhibit and found a plaque reading "Confederate Currency: The Color of Money."

Dozens of these paintings lined the walls, and displayed between the paintings was actual currency used by the Confederacy. The Confederate States of America put pictures of happy, fully clothed slaves wearing shoes on their money because they knew that the currency traveled around the world. It was southern propaganda in the era before television, tweets, and Facebook.

The King Center also displayed copies of the secession ordinances. The state of Mississippi spelled out its reasons for seceding from the Union: "Our position is thoroughly identified with the institution of slavery—the greatest material interest of the world. . . . A blow at slavery is a blow at commerce and civilization." This helps explain why member states of the Confederacy put slaves on the money they printed. For them, enslaved people equaled money. To lose the people was to lose money—too much to still be able to maintain their way of life.

As I stared at the secession ordinances, I remembered our first stop on the pilgrimage: Dahlonega, Georgia, the site of the first American gold rush. It was Cherokee land and had been for nearly thirteen thousand years. The Cherokee Nation signed a dozen treaties with the United States between 1795 and 1819 in attempts to protect the land and the people. The 1820s were a time of great promise for the Cherokee Nation.[2] In that decade the Nation developed its own written syllabary, drafted its own constitution, and established its capital city: New Echota, in Georgia.

But in 1828, a little Cherokee boy found gold. The same year, Georgia began passing laws stripping the Cherokees of their lands and rights. Within years, miners moved in and—without permission—set up camps on Cherokee territory. In 1830, President Andrew Jackson signed the Indian Removal Act, which gave him power to negotiate removal treaties with tribes living east of the Mississippi River. At the same time, the state of Georgia divided the Cherokee Nation's land into lots for the miners.

In 1831, the Nation asked the US Supreme Court to grant an injunction against Georgia's punitive laws. The court ruled that it lacked the proper jurisdiction to take the case. A group of missionaries, including Samuel Austin Worcester, later exercised civil disobedience by refusing to obtain a state license to occupy Cherokee lands. In essence, they thumbed their nose at the state's right to rule over Cherokee land. The missionaries were jailed. Cherokee Chief John Ross took their case to the US Supreme Court and won. In *Worcester v. Georgia,* the court ruled that the Cherokee Nation was a sovereign nation. As such, the state of Georgia did not have the right to impose regulations on the Nation; only the federal government had that authority.[3]

Still, by the end of 1838 and in defiance of the US Supreme Court, President Jackson's coerced treaties had resulted in the removal of nearly forty-six thousand Cherokee, Chickasaw, Creek, Choctaw, and Seminole men, women, and children. The illegal deportation cleared twenty-five million acres of land for white settlement, mining, and ultimately slavery.[4] The US Branch Mint at Dahlonega opened for business and produced its first gold coins the same year.[5]

As I reflected on Dahlonega while standing in front of the Confederate currency exhibit in the King Center, a thought hit me. *This is the Bible Belt.* These things happened at the hands of people who claimed to believe in Jesus and the power of the Cross for salvation. How could they believe the gospel and do this?

WHAT IS THE GOSPEL?

Two years later I was speaking to a group of college ministry staff. "What is the gospel?" I asked them. This was a particularly provocative question for these staff members, who were expert at communicating the good news of the gospel as it had been handed down to them. They knew all manner of frameworks and diagrams to make the message simple. But beneath the surface of their successful frameworks, a void occupied the center of the message.

What exactly *was* Jesus's "good news"?

The group formed four teams to examine the New Testament gospels: one examined Mark, another explored Matthew, another dissected Luke, and the last investigated John. They had twenty minutes to discern each gospel writer's understanding of the good news.

When time was up, this diverse group of men and women came back together to share what they had discovered. These accomplished ministry staff members were amazed. The good news of the gospel writers was not quite the good news they had been preaching. The gospel writers' vision was much bigger.

The team members found that Matthew, Mark, Luke, and John all cared about an individual's reconciliation with God, self, and their communities. But the gospel writers also focused on systemic justice, peace between people groups, and freedom for the oppressed. The good news was both about the *coming* of the Kingdom of God and the *character* of that Kingdom. It was about what God's Kingdom looked like. It was about what citizenship in God's Kingdom requires. The biblical gospel writers' good news was about the restoration of shalom..

THE DIVIDED GOSPEL

The Second Great Awakening swept over America at the peak of King Cotton's reign in the South. Heightened global demand for cotton collided with the invention of the cotton gin and the abolition of the Atlantic slave trade. Far greater numbers of slaves were needed to pick and process cotton, but Africans were no longer being brought to America. To address the need for more free labor, slave owners began breeding their own slaves.

The slave population in the United States exploded from seven hundred thousand in 1790 to nearly four million by 1860. The impact on gospel proclamation? Charles Finney, the leading revivalist of the nineteenth century, created the altar call to give people the chance to stand up and walk forward, proclaiming that they were aligning themselves with the Kingdom of God. But citizenship in the Kingdom of God, Finney insisted, required allegiance to God's governance over and above any human governance, including the social, legal, and economic institution of slavery. Men and women confessed and repented of their personal sins as well as their complicity with structural evil. And when they wiped away their tears and opened their eyes, Finney thrust a pen into their hands and pointed them to sign-up sheets for the abolitionist movement. This is what it meant to be an evangelical Christian in the 1800s.

Church historian David Bebbington has identified four characteristics common to American evangelicals during the birthing period of the movement:

1. Conversionism. The belief that all humanity is called by God to move from a state of darkness into light, to be transformed as we convert from living as subjects of the kingdom of this world to living as subjects of the Kingdom of God.

2. Activism. The conviction that it is not enough to believe a particular set of principles or doctrines. Rather, principles and doctrines must transform the way we live. Our faith is kinetic, lived out in the world through our hands and feet.

3. Biblicism. The belief that the Bible is the ultimate authority, period.

4. Crucicentrism. The belief that Jesus's death on the cross stands at the center of our faith. On the cross Jesus died and became sin itself. The transformative power of the Cross offers the world the power to be transformed from sin and death into life.[6]

These characteristics marked the common commitments of evangelicals throughout the nineteenth century. But industrialization in the North produced a new type of inhumane servitude. Baptist minister Walter Rauschenbusch witnessed the impact of the Industrial Revolution at the turn of the twentieth century. A river of former farmers flowed into poverty-infested tenements in the Hell's Kitchen area of New York City. Men, women, and children—including members of Rauschenbusch's Second German Baptist Church—were forced to work twelve-hour days in horrific conditions. Disease, malnutrition, and death were commonplace.[7]

Rauschenbusch realized the early twentieth-century church had lost its focus on the Kingdom of God. He called out the church's complicity in condoning common rationalizations for the evils of the Industrial Revolution. People were said to be poor because they wanted to be poor or because they lacked strength of character. Rauschenbusch challenged this thinking:

Single cases of unhappiness are inevitable in our frail human life; but when there are millions of them, all running along well-defined grooves, reducible to certain laws, then this misery is not an individual, but a social matter, due to causes in the structure of our society and curable only by social reconstruction.[8]

People didn't want to live in poverty. Rather, members of Rauschen-busch's congregation—and millions of others—were caught in well-defined grooves carved out by oppressive systems, not their own character flaws.

Workers were moving through a systematic assembly line that led to destitution. To combat such widespread injustice, Rauschenbusch called the church to return to the Scriptures. The Scriptures are not silent on struc-tural and systemic sin. The Bible overflows with God's responses to poverty, oppression, and governance.[9]

In response, the small but growing fundamentalist movement rose up in ire, declaring that Rauschenbusch had muddied the gospel message. Fundamentalist Christians argued that the gospel was about one thing only: Christ crucified as payment for our individual sins. Thus began the church's own civil war, which notably took place within the white Ameri-can church.

The white American church split in two from 1908 through the 1920s. Rauschenbusch's followers were called Modernists (known today as the lib-eral church). The conservative faction launched the Fundamentalist move-ment, under the leadership of people such as Cyrus (C. I.) Scofield, whose work is widely known today through the Scofield Bible. The Fundamental-ists also founded seminaries, including Dallas Theological Seminary and Westminster Theological Seminary.

In the 1940s, a subset of the Fundamentalist movement became known as evangelicals, named after the nineteenth-century movement. However, they didn't adopt the early movement's expansive call for personal *and* structural repentance. Instead, they maintained a strict Fundamentalist focus on personal repentance from personal imperfection, which led to per-sonal salvation.

Throughout the twentieth century, the liberal church largely distanced itself from calls to personal piety and a passionate, personal relationship with God. Instead, many historic white Protestant churches fought against systemic justice. Some partnered with the historic black church. Others partnered with labor unions to fight the exploitation of labor and were early proponents of women's rights.

Meanwhile, twentieth-century evangelicals took up the cause of evangelism. They spread the good news of personal salvation. And in the latter part of the century, charismatic evangelicals experienced healing encounters with the Spirit of God. A great chasm opened, splitting the gospel in two. On both sides of the divide, the gospel was thinner than before, containing only a fraction of its power and of God's purposes for the world.

THIN VERSUS THICK FAITH

Gospel tracts, simple diagrams, and fill-in-the-blank studies have created what theologian Miroslav Volf calls "thin faith."[10] Thin religion lacks deep roots in the Scriptures and Christian traditions. It skims the surface of sacred texts, using what seems applicable in the moment without connecting the dots. To overcome thin faith, Christians need to study Scripture in light of the writers' historic and cultural contexts, the original meanings of words, and the biblical text in the context of the teachings of church fathers and mothers. It requires serious study and reflection.

In contrast, thin faith rests on "what my pastor said" or "what this Bible passage says to me" (without contextual study), or it doesn't reference sacred texts at all. Thin faith creates its own collection of Instagram memes that serve as life principles. One's personal point of view becomes the highest authority. Because thin faith lacks roots, it can be swept away, manipulated, and even marginalized so that it has no bearing on the private or public lives of the faithful. Witness politicians who claim faith when they are trying to get elected. If they have only a vague idea of what the sacred texts actually say, their post-election decisions are likely to bear little resemblance to thick faith.

> Thin faith creates its own collection of Instagram memes that serve as life principles.

For more than a century now, thinned-out faith has left the divided American church struggling to grasp the significance of the prophetic voices among us. It also has left us without the biblical foundations needed to comprehend Kingdom theology. What we need is a thicker approach to the central question of our faith: what is the good news of the gospel?

SHALOM

The word *shalom* in all of its forms appears frequently in the Bible. It is used 550 times.[11]

The five forms of the word are as follows:

- *shalom,* a Hebrew noun that means peace and wholeness— used 225 times.
- *shalem,* a Hebrew verb that means to make right and to restore—used 117 times.
- *shelem,* a Hebrew noun that means peace offering—used 87 times.
- *shalem,* also a Hebrew adjective that means loyal or devoted— used 27 times.
- *eirene,* a Greek noun that means peace—used 94 times.

In Scripture, the word *shalom* itself means

- well-being
- wholeness
- the perfection of God's creation
- abundance
- peace

It is used as a greeting that wishes right relationships in community for the recipient of the blessing (see Genesis 29:6; 2 Kings 4:26; Jeremiah 15:5). It also is used to bless the dying with a charge to "go to your ancestors" (Genesis 15:15; see 1 Kings 2:6) and as a promise of safe passage and safe conduct (see Judges 18:6; Psalm 4:8).

Shalom describes the absence of conflict (see Deuteronomy 2:26; Isaiah 33:7) and is used in the context of prophesies of salvation for the vulnerable and condemnation for the unjust (see Jeremiah 6:14; Micah 3:5; Zechariah 9:10). It also is used in the contexts of prayer and politics (see Psalm 72:7; 85:8, 10).

In the New Testament, the Greek form of shalom (*eirene*) is used ninety-four times and means restoration of relationship, wholeness, healing, and peace. A word used in Matthew 5:9, *eireneopoios,* means "those who do peace" or shalom doers.

Luke 1:79 speaks of a "way of peace"—an ethic of eirene.

John 14:26–27 contrasts eirene and fear.

Acts 9:31 reveals that eirene is for all people (Judea, Galilee, and Samaria). Shalom living involves the fear of the Lord and the comfort of the Holy Spirit and leads to church growth.

Paul uses *eirene* in all his letters, and the word is used in all but one of the remainder of the New Testament epistles.

While the word *shalom* is not used in Genesis 1 or 2, these chapters give us two of the most vivid pictures of shalom in Scripture. In these texts, we see one of the central concepts of shalom—we are all connected—lived out.

The peace of self is dependent upon the peace of the other. God created the world in a web of relationships that overflowed with forceful goodness. These relationships are far-reaching: between humanity and God, between humanity and self, between genders, between humanity and the rest of creation, within families, between ethnic groups or races, and between nations. These relationships were "very good" in the beginning. One word characterized them all: *shalom.* Then the story of the Fall (see Genesis 3) explains how the relationships were broken. The rest of Scripture takes us on a journey toward redemption and restoration.

Shalom is the stuff of the Kingdom. It's what the Kingdom of God looks like in context. It's what citizenship in the Kingdom of God requires and what the Kingdom promises to those who choose God and God's ways to peace.

To live in God's Kingdom, in the way of shalom, requires that we discard our thin understanding of the gospel. I had to face a

> The peace of self is dependent upon the peace of the other.

hard truth: my limited, evangelical understanding of the gospel had nothing to say about sixteen thousand Cherokees and four other sovereign indigenous nations whose people were forcibly removed from their lands. And it had nothing to say to my own ancestors who were enslaved in South Carolina.

My personal pilgrimage has continued for thirteen years. In that time, I have been working out my understanding of shalom and its implications for my life, my practice of the gospel, and my work as a Christian justice advocate. I have preached, trained, and written. I have organized faith communities to fight various manifestations of oppression and brokenness. In previous books and lectures, I have explored the significance of shalom when it is brought to bear on public policy and the common good. I also have preached and written on shalom and the problems of shame, family brokenness, domestic abuse, and global witness. I have come to understand a few things that will be fleshed out in the chapters that follow:

1. If one's gospel falls mute when facing people who need good news the most—the impoverished, the oppressed, and the broken—then it's no gospel at all.

2. Shalom is what the Kingdom of God smells like. It's what the Kingdom looks like and what Jesus requires of the Kingdom's citizens. It's when everyone has enough. It's when families are healed. It's when shame is renounced and inner freedom is laid hold of. It's when human dignity, bestowed by the image of God in all humanity, is cultivated, protected, and served in families, faith communities, and schools and through public policy. Shalom is when the capacity to lead is recognized in every human being and when nations join together to protect the environment.

3. At its heart, the biblical concept of shalom is about God's vision for the emphatic goodness of all relationships. In his book *Peace,* Walter Brueggemann wrote, "The vision of wholeness, which is the supreme will of the biblical God, is the outgrowth of a covenant of *shalom* (see Ezekiel 34:25), in which persons are bound not only to God but to one another in a caring, sharing, rejoicing community with none to make them afraid."[12]

So what is the vision? What was God's original intent for our world and all the relationships within it? What did God call good? What is the goodness that God is working to restore?

As we begin this journey to live in the shalom of God's Kingdom, I remember the words of my former pastor Dr. Ron Benefiel at the Los Angeles First Church of the Nazarene. He would stand before the congregation on Sunday morning and say, "I'm just a beggar, sharing with other beggars where I've found food."

Well, I've found food. Want some?

A Glimpse of Shalom

In the beginning, two divine beings ruled: Apsu (fresh waters) and his wife, Tiamat (salty waters). The two swirled together and the waters became one. And within their waters, demons, monsters, and gods were birthed. Violence, death, and chaos ruled the surging waters as Apsu and Tiamat's progeny warred against one another. Apsu and Tiamat plotted to kill their children so that peace might be restored, but their great-grandson Ea rose up and killed Apsu.

Spitting rage and vengeance, Tiamat created eleven monsters to help her win the battle against her descendants. Tiamat's new lover, the god Kingu, led her army, and her progeny were terrified. Then Ea's son, the storm god Marduk, rose up and promised to defeat her on one condition: if he prevailed, he would reign supreme. He won.

In his first act of supremacy, Marduk split Tiamat in two. Her ribs became the dome of the sky and the soil of the earth, her pierced eyes became the source of the Tigris and Euphrates Rivers, and her tail became the Milky Way. Then Marduk took the blood of Kingu, mixed it with the red clay earth, and made humankind—to serve the gods forever.

Before there was Genesis 1, there was *Enuma Elish,* this Babylonian creation story. Most scholars believe that Genesis 1 was the last of four sections of the Pentateuch to be written down. Genesis is the youngest of the first five books of the Bible, likely written just after the fall of the Babylonian Empire and the end of the exilic period (ca. 538–450 BCE).

At this time, the Hebrew people—having been utterly conquered—were about to reestablish the nation of Israel. In this context, the priests who wrote Genesis 1 were likely attempting to wash off the cultural and spiritual rags of seventy years of captivity by reinterpreting the Hebrew creation story while commenting on their oppressor's narrative. The Babylonian creation story of Enuma Elish, commonly called the Babylonian Genesis, would have been a familiar story to the people. It had been used by the Babylonians to reinforce their cultural, social, and political dominance over the Hebrews.

The Genesis 1 authors, priests who were Babylonian exiles, compiled generations of priestly oral tradition to write the text.[1] In verse 1 we encounter God. There was none who came before God. The context of all things is God—a direct affront to the Babylonian theological worldview.

In verse 2 we see that the earth is "a formless [*tohuw*] void and darkness [*choshek*] covered the face of the deep [*thowm*]." The Hebrew word *tohuw* (formless) means "a desolation." From this we see that apart from God the world is not neutral. It is emphatically negative, a desolation. What's more, it is vacuous. Then, in the same sentence, it gets worse: "darkness covered the face of the deep." The Hebrew word *choshek* (darkness) means exactly that: darkness. Its figurative meaning is misery, destruction, death, ignorance, sorrow, wickedness, and the list goes on. The priests painted a picture of emphatic agony. Were they providing a commentary on the state of the people of Israel surrounded by Babylonian corruption, repression, and desolation? Much like the waters mentioned in Enuma Elish, the deep in Genesis is full of agony. But in the Genesis story there are no smaller gods. There is only the one God: Elohim. Elohim does not come from the deep; Elohim is separate from and independent of the chaos and agony of oppression.

The earth, however, is a vacuous desolation. It is a surging mass of water surrounded by misery, destruction, death, sorrow. And then . . . action!

The wind, the breath, the violent exhalation of God moves over this surging mass of misery. The Hebrew word for move literally means to brood, as a hen broods over her eggs. It is as if God's spirit— *ruwach,* a feminine noun in Hebrew—positions herself to confront the misery and destruction, the sorrow and wickedness. She broods over it as if she is about to do battle with the darkness. Her strategy for engagement is birth—new life.

Then Elohim, the supreme God, speaks: "Let there be light!" (Genesis 1:3). And light is born. "And [Elohim] saw that the light was good" (verse 4). The voice and command of God birth light. There is clarity. There is happiness. God speaks and goodness is birthed from a cesspool of despair.

This is our human context. We are surrounded by the stuff of darkness. It weaves destruction into our lives and our world, and it is utterly painful.

But God!

You see? The darkness is real! It is utterly chaotic, truly destructive. But God is positioned over it and confronts the darkness. The authors of Genesis 1 were emphatic about the utter desolation of our world before God spoke. But when God spoke, it changed everything!

> We are surrounded by the stuff of darkness. It weaves destruction into our lives and our world, and it is utterly painful.

A Need to Hear from God

It's not hard to see where we need God to speak. As I wrote this chapter, ISIL (Islamic State of Iraq and Levant) was wreaking havoc. Having taken advantage of a destabilized Syria, ISIL claimed the state as its own, forcing millions of Syrians to flee. Syrian refugees exceeded the capacity of refugee camps all over the Middle East and moved throughout Europe in the largest migration of displaced persons since World War II.[2]

Meanwhile, terrorist rampages in Paris and San Bernardino, California, took place less than three weeks apart in late 2015. ISIL claimed responsibility for the Paris and San Bernardino massacres. Some European countries most affected by the refugee crisis continued to welcome refugees fleeing ISIL, but many rejected them. And thirty-one governors of states in the United States declared they would not accept refugees.[3]

Is there any question that the world needs to hear from God?

On the domestic front in 2015, 40 percent of unarmed people killed by police were black men, yet black men make up only 6 percent of the national population.[4] Americans witnessed a rise in the activities of white supremacist groups as well. Churches were set afire across the South and Midwest after governors removed Confederate flags from state grounds following the racist massacre of nine black men and women during a prayer meeting at Emanuel African Methodist Episcopal Church in Charleston, South Carolina. In the final weeks of 2015, members of a white-supremacist group fired into a crowd of young people as they protested the police killing of Jamar Clark in Minneapolis, Minnesota. We need to hear from God.

Consider also that from 1999 to 2013, the fatality rate rose far above the average number in the middle-aged white demographic. An increase of

more than a half million men and women died due to suicide, drug over-
dose, and alcoholism. This is a blaring indicator of the silent suffering of a
demographic in need of hope.[5]

All of this is set against a backdrop of critical social issues affecting individuals and families. Shame, broken and estranged families, gangs, economic inequality, and rising rates of cancer are prominent in the chaos of
our world. We need to hear from God.

The authors of Genesis 1 invite us to understand that Elohim, by Elohim's nature, is positioned over and against the darkness in our lives and
our world. All Elohim needs to do is speak and light will come. Elohim
separates light from darkness and names the light "Day" and the darkness
"Night." This took place on day one, in the first act of creation. It's important to note that God does not obliterate the darkness; rather, God names it
and limits it—puts boundaries on it. The boundary is the light. The priests
who survived seventy years of oppression in Babylon understood something
about the darkness and the boundary that is set by light. They waited and
raised multiple generations under Babylonian rule, but the light came. The
exile ended; they were allowed to return to their homeland.

African Americans celebrate Juneteenth, the oldest celebration of the
day black people were set free from slavery in the United States. Two years
after President Lincoln's Emancipation Proclamation, Union soldiers
marched into Galveston, Texas. They spread the news that the Civil War
was over and the people were free. The Hebrew word for "light" (*'owr*) in
the Genesis text can be translated as "happiness." I imagine that on June 19,
1865, there was uncontrollable happiness. In the same way, the priests and
the Hebrew people crossed over the boundary of their Babylonian suffering
when they walked back to their homeland.

This is the promise of Genesis 1. The darkness is limited by the light. Suffering is not in perpetuity. The light may take generations to come, but it will come. There is always hope.

We long for a world without pain, sorrow, and death. But in the beginning, when God could have rid the world of misery, God did not choose to do so. God's governance is positioned against destruction, wickedness, and all things that cause misery. And though God does not eliminate the darkness, God exercises mercy by placing boundaries on it. In God's Kingdom, darkness does not overcome. The light always breaks through!

> The light may take generations to come, but it will come.

I have a beautiful friend named Barbara, who has endured incredible pain. She witnessed her mother's death in a house fire. It would be easy for Barbara to be consumed by this gruesome memory. It would be easy for her to become paralyzed by the chaos of the deep. But, instead, each morning Barbara thanks God for the light by reviewing her list of one thousand things she is thankful for and adding to it. In that way, she beats back the darkness and enters every day surrounded by gratitude and light.

In Genesis 1, we read again and again these three phrases: "Let . . . ," "and it was so," and "God saw that it was good." These phrases are repeated from the first verse of Genesis 1 to the last. When we read them, we sense a reinforcement of the truth that God is supreme ruler. What God commands happens.

Over the next four days described in Genesis, God continues to separate out domains. First it is light from darkness, then the waters below from the heavens and the sky, then the land from the sea. These are the domains from which life will spring. Then Elohim calls forth vegetation from the land, swarms of living creatures from the waters, birds for the air, and animals of every kind to walk and crawl upon the earth. And God places the sun, moon, and stars in the sky to rule over the day and night.

GOD CREATED SEA MONSTERS

Two things regarding God's governance are worth noting. First is that the principal outcome of God's governance is goodness and, second, that Elohim created sea monsters.

The ancients were deathly afraid of the sea, the place where sea monsters lived. In the Enuma Elish fables, Tiamat creates eleven sea monsters. Other ancient poems speak of gods rising up against sea monsters. The sea was a mysterious place of great struggle, loss, and fear. Yet in God's governance, God did not eliminate the source of fear and worry. Rather, just as Elohim did on the first day when darkness was limited by the boundary of light, God called forth the land to place boundaries on the deep.

The writers of Genesis make a point to highlight one being that God created on the fifth day: the sea monster. Why are sea monsters so significant? In one sense, the priestly writers seem to poke fun at the gods of Babylon. Tiamat created sea monsters for vengeance in the midst of a war for supremacy. Here, in the Hebrew creation story, Elohim created them as an act of goodness—and he blessed them!

In another sense, if Elohim created sea monsters, then God is above the peoples' greatest source of fear in the same way that the Spirit of God was positioned over the deep. We are not subject to the worst the deep has to offer. Rather, the waters and every creature in them are subject to God.

The Hebrew people knew from experience that even Babylon was subject to God. They had been set free from the sea monsters of the Babylonian Empire.

In Genesis, Elohim calls every creature in the sea and the air (including sea monsters) good. It is good that the waters and the sea monsters are part of God's creation. It is good that the sea monsters' presence drives people to trust God. It is good that when we encounter Babylons in our lives and in our world, we are driven back into the protective care of Elohim, the supreme God over all creation, the One who beats back the darkness. God provides for the needs of all; God speaks and it is so; God governs for the good of all.

The text reaches its climax midway through the sixth day. On this day Elohim speaks three words and a phrase that I believe provide the essence of the vision of shalom: image (*tselem*), likeness (*dmuwth*), dominion (*radah*), and very good (*tov me'od*).

Three Words and a Phrase at the Heart of Shalom

Elohim, supreme Creator, has separated out the domains and brought forth every plant and living creature on earth. Next, God said, "Let us make humankind in our image [*tselem*], according to our likeness [*dmuwth*]; and let them have dominion [*radah*] over the fish of the sea, and over the birds of the air, and over the cattle, and over all the wild animals of the earth, and over every creeping thing that creeps upon the earth" (Genesis 1:26).

The word *tselem* is repeated three times within two verses. Because the ancients did not have bold, italics, or underlining at their disposal, writers often relied on the power of repetition to indicate the significance of a word, thought, or concept. *Tselem* literally means "a phantom." Figuratively, it means "representative figure." This is a bold, even revolutionary, challenge to the dominant view regarding who represented God on earth. At that time, only kings and queens were considered representatives of deity.

In direct opposition to the prevailing view, the writers of Genesis 1 democratize dignity by redistributing it to all humanity. And humanity does not inherit its intrinsic worth and dignity on the basis of bloodline, financial status, or royal position. Rather, dignity and worth are inherited from humanity's creator, Elohim, the supreme God. We are made in the likeness (*dmuwth*) of Elohim, just as children are made in the likeness of their parents.

The word *tselem* is also the Hebrew form of the Greek word *eikon*. Think *icon*. Jesus used the word *eikon* to describe the graven image of Caesar on a Roman coin. "'Why are you putting me to the test, you hypocrites? Show me the coin used for the tax.' And they brought him a denarius. Then he said to them, 'Whose head [*eikon*] is this, and whose title?' They answered, 'The emperor's'" (Matthew 22:18–21). The word *eikon* was used in New Testament times to describe the image of Caesar in great statues erected at city gates, in his face engraved on coins, and in images and symbols of Caesar throughout the empire. The *eikon* of Caesar was meant to declare to subjects, "Caesar rules here!"

Jesus continued speaking about the coin and Caesar's image: "Give therefore to the emperor the things that are the emperor's, and to God the things that are God's" (verse 21). The coin bears the *eikon* of Caesar, it is Caesar's. But what bears God's *eikon*? I do. You do.

According to the writers of Genesis 1, Elohim has imprinted every human being with the *tselem* of God. All humanity bears God's image.

Because humanity belongs to God, one of our functions is to serve as markers of where God rules.

The implications are immense. The priests of the post-exilic period were speaking to a recently oppressed people. They had lived in a land where the theological worldview told them they existed to serve gods who were merciless, vengeful, and brutal. Their gods treated the Babylonians as if they were no more than pawns in a game, so how much more oppressively would the gods have acted toward the Hebrews? But the doctrine of the image of God reversed all that. The priests reminded the Hebrews of their profound intrinsic worth and dignity.

The homeless man on a street corner today is made in the image of God. The Colombian worker making two cents per day on a multinational company's cocoa farm is made in the image of God. Farm workers and domestic workers, who are exempt from basic workers' rights in the United States, are made in the image of God. Amadou Diallo, Trayvon Martin, Jordan Davis, Rekia Boyd, Michael Brown, Ezell Ford, John Crawford III, Eric Garner, Tamir Rice, Yvette Smith, Freddie Gray, the Mother Emanuel Nine, Sandra Bland, India Kager, Jamar Clark, Laquan McDonald, and other unarmed victims of police and vigilante killings are made in the image of God. Women and men who are systematically pushed to the margins of society possess as much dignity and worth as Hillary Clinton, Jeb Bush, Oprah Winfrey, Angelina Jolie, and any other people who are esteemed like royalty in our culture.

We are not God. But because we bear God's image, we are worthy of human dignity, love, respect, honor, and protection.

And there is more! In Genesis 1, God continues, "And let them have dominion [*radah*] over the fish of the sea, and over the birds of the air, and over the cattle, and over all the wild animals of the earth, and over every creeping thing that creeps upon the earth" (verse 26). We are created for dominion!

GOD CALLS US TO EXERCISE DOMINION

God makes humankind in God's image and in the same breath calls humanity to exercise dominion (*radah*). Theological arguments abound for what it means to be made in the image of God. Some say it means we have characteristics that are like God's. We are creative beings and have feelings. We are created for community like that shared within the Trinity. While all of this is true, I do not see the text itself making these connections. Rather, within the text the Hebrew word *tselem* (representative figure) is linked directly to human dominion (*radah*). What it means to be made in the image of God is seen in the call and capacity of all humanity to exercise dominion.

When we think of the word *dominion*, images of European royalty, Chinese emperors, and Egyptian pharaohs likely come to mind. It's understandable that dominion would be associated with the human exercise of power and rule, including imperialism and the exploitation of land and people.

The image seared into my mind is that of Henry VIII as portrayed in the hit television show *The Tudors*. Henry ruled by deception, manipulation, and brute retaliation for perceived and actual insurrection and ultimately was most concerned with his legacy rather than the well-being of his people and neighboring nations. This form of dominion forces weaker subjects to bend to the will of empire or be broken. But Genesis 1 paints a picture of God's rule that bears little similarity to the human exercise of power and earthly rule.

In addition to *radah*, eight other Hebrew words are used in Scripture to connote the English word *dominion*. In Genesis alone, two words in addition to *radah* are used for dominion. *Mashal,* used in Genesis 37:8, means "to rule, govern." This is a reference to the power that makes it possible to govern. And in Genesis 27:40, *ruwd* means "to tramp about or ramble." In this passage, Isaac prophesies to Esau, saying, "By your sword you shall live, and you shall serve your brother; but when you break loose [*ruwd*], you shall break his yoke from your neck." In other words, this reference isn't about governing or empire at all; it's about breaking free.

The authors of Genesis 1 could have used as many as eight other words if they had wanted to communicate that dominion means to rule creation in the same way a king rules an empire. But instead, they chose *radah,* a primitive root word that means "to tread down or subjugate." It also can mean to rule, but even then it conveys the sense that one rules as the result of winning a struggle. *Radah* is not a call to exercise imperial power.

Think about this. The writers of Genesis 1 had just described the beginning of the world—the first trees, first plants, first animals, the first everything. And within creation, Elohim set the boundaries of each domain. In all of creation, the separate parts have relationships that operate well within their boundaries. Beyond that, God has ordained relationships between each of the domains of creation.

The writers' use of *radah* conjures images of a new creation in need of stewardship. For you and me, the image of an untamed wilderness is an appropriate reference point.

THE SUBSTANCE OF GOD'S KIND OF PEACE

July 2004, I boarded a bus in Sarajevo, Bosnia, along with twenty-five other students and staff of a college ministry. I was co-leading a journey that took us across Croatia, into Serbia, and through Bosnia. We wanted to learn more about the substance of God's kind of peace: how is it built and how is it broken? As we traveled on Bosnia's main highway, we saw home after home so riddled with bullets they were badly damaged. Historically, prime targets in a war are government buildings, arsenals, factories, railroads, bridges, and military installations. But during the Bosnian war, Serbian forces made it their mission to "kill the homes." Now, ten years later, we passed house after house riddled with bullet holes, and trees were growing up through the bombed-out houses. When humanity does not fulfill its call to steward creation, the untamed wilderness takes over.

Stewardship requires agency: the use of one's voice to guide and direct and the use of one's mind to make choices that impact the world. The post-exilic Hebrews

> Ten years later, we passed house after house riddled with bullet holes, and trees were growing up through the bombed-out houses.

had endured several generations as captives, having lost the freedom to use their voice as well as the power of making choices. Now, as the priests are writing Genesis 1, they are in the process of rebuilding the Temple: the seat of Hebrew power.

Whole generations had never known freedom. They had no idea what it meant to exercise agency. I'm sure there were some who had heard the stories of the elders, recalling life before captivity. Having now returned to the land of Israel, the most ambitious Hebrews would likely seek to restore their dignity through position and power.

That was the context within which the priestly writers of Genesis 1 declared that all humanity is created with the call and the capacity to exercise dominion. *Radah* equalizes power. No one is too low to exercise agency to steward God's creation. Likewise, no one can add value to his or her soul through the pursuit and exercise of power. We all are equally powerful, and we all are equally vulnerable. The call to exercise *radah* would have been both subversive and humbling for post-exilic Hebrews.

At this point in the text, the priestly writers can no longer contain their emotion. They break into song. Using a classic A-B-B-A structure, they sing the point of it all and add a revolutionary zinger:

> So God created humankind [A] in his image [B],
>   in the image of God [B] he created them [A];
>   male and female he created them. [zinger!] (Genesis 1:27)

Imagine how this would have been received by the original hearers. The writers challenge the culturally entrenched Hebrew worldview that defines women as property. In their song, the writers declare that both men and women are made in the image of God. Both men and women are born with inherent dignity and worth. Women bear the image of God equally, with no distinction in the way that image is manifest. They share equally in the call to exercise dominion.

And so we come to the fourth word at the core of the vision.

INDEED IT WAS VERY GOOD

At the end of the sixth day, the writers declare, "God saw everything that he had made, and indeed, it was very good [*tov me'od*]. And there was evening and there was morning, the sixth day" (Genesis 1:31).

Tov is the Hebrew word for "good," but the word does not refer only to the goodness of the object itself; it also refers to the ties between things. In the Hebrew conception of the world, all of creation is connected. The well-being of the whole depends on the well-being of each individual part. The Hebrews' conception of goodness was different than the Greeks'. The Greeks located perfection within the object itself. A thing or a person strove toward perfection. But the Hebrews understood goodness to be located *between* things. As a result, the original hearers would have understood *tov* to refer to the goodness of the ties and relationships between things in creation.[6]

Me'od is an adjective that means "forceful" or "vehement." Biblical scholar Terry McGonigal has added to that definition: "abundant, flourishing, overflowing, and never ending." McGonigal also explained that *tov* appears six times previously in this text. Here, the seventh time it is used, the word describes God's creation, and the writers add the emphatic adjective *me'od*. In Hebrew culture, the numbers seven and ten symbolize perfection. The fact that the writers add *me'od* on the seventh occurrence of the word is significant. McGonigal holds that this usage indicates the writers are communicating the completeness and perfect interconnectedness of the web of creation. It is *tov me'od* because all the relationships between things overflow with goodness!

The original hearers and readers of Genesis 1 would have understood that the writers were not merely saying that each part of God's creation was very good but rather that God's mighty web of interconnected relationships was forcefully good, vehemently good, abundantly good!

The relationship between humanity and God was forcefully good.

Humanity's relationship with self was forcefully good.

The relationship between humanity and the rest of creation was forcefully good.

The relationship between men and women was forcefully good.

The relationship within the first community—the community of creation (God, humanity, and the rest of creation)—was forcefully good.

The relationship between humanity and the systems that govern (the way things worked) was forcefully good.

And the relationship between humanity and life itself was forcefully good.

It is forcefully good that God is supreme and distinct from humanity. It is forcefully good that the darkness has the boundary of the light. It is forcefully good that the sun, moon, and stars help people know when to sleep and when to wake, when to sow and when to reap. It is abundantly good that the fear-inducing surging waters are limited by the land. And it is utterly good that the sea monsters drive humanity back into God's caring arms. It is vehemently good that humanity is made in the image of God, each soul carrying inherent dignity and the call and capacity to steward the rest of creation. It is beautifully good that Elohim provided for the needs of all creation, including humans and beasts and everything with breath that was given vegetables for food.

In the end, we see that God's governance has transformed the world from a cesspool of overwhelming darkness, despair, sorrow, misery, destruction, and death into a world where darkness is limited by the light. Where Elohim is supreme over the waters and all that live in them. Where goodness springs forth from the commands of God. And where the relationships between all things are *tov me'od*!

The implications of the vision are profound:

- *All humanity is made in the image of God.* To slap another human is to slap the image of God. To lie to another human is to lie to the image of God. To exploit another human is to exploit the image of God. To kill another human is to kill the image of God. To declare war on another human or an ethnic group or a religion or a nation is to declare war on the image of God. In essence, to commit acts of physical, emotional, psychological, sexual, political, and economic violence against fellow humans is to attempt to crush the image of God on earth. Likewise, to exploit or harm or overconsume the rest of creation is to abdicate our human vocation—to steward creation. If we engage in such acts, we turn our backs on God's way to peace and, by extension, on God.

- *All humanity is created with the call and capacity to exercise dominion.* The young Somali cab driver is created with the call and the capacity to exercise dominion. The woman stocking shelves at Walmart is created with the call and capacity to exercise dominion. The child in an under-resourced public school with no books, lockers, or music class is created with the call and capacity to exercise dominion. The 2.5 million men and women languishing in our criminal justice system are created with the call and capacity to exercise dominion. Even when that potential is buried by poverty or sickness or corrupted by violence, the call remains in force. God created all of us with the ability to steward our world.

- *To diminish the capacity of humans to exercise dominion is to diminish the image of God on earth.* This is why governance is so important—not only governance of nations, states, and cities but also governance of businesses, homes, relationships, and our very selves. These are the realms we govern and the relationships we were created to steward. As we steward well, in a way that reflects God's kind of stewardship, the image of God flourishes. When we steward poorly, the image of God suffers and is ultimately diminished on earth.

- *If humanity is created in God's likeness, then the way we exercise dominion should reflect God's kind of dominion.* It should maintain the overwhelming well-being of all. It should not seek to advance or privilege one's self. To exercise dominion that seeks one's own well-being first is to break from the likeness of God.

Reflection Exercise

Let's do a relationship governance inventory.

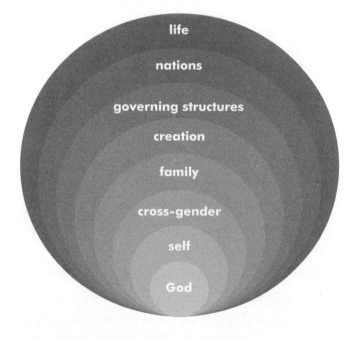

Think of your life as having concentric circles of relationships. In the innermost circle, place your relationship with God. In the next ring is your relationship with self. In the next circle out, consider your cross-gender relationships. In the next circle, consider your relationships with family members, spouse, close friends, and colleagues. In the next circle out, think about your relationships with the land and the rest of creation. Consider where the closest green space is in your life. Do you live in a city, a suburb, a small town, or the country? When was the last time you took a walk outdoors? Do you grow your own food? Do you own pets? What energy resources do you rely on most?

In the next circle out, consider governing structures such as your city council, the school board, state representatives, your governor, and the policies that come from these offices. There is another kind of governing structure as well: businesses. Just as voters influence state governance in a democracy, shareholders and consumers influence the public impacts of businesses in capitalist society. Consider, are you a voter or a legislator? Are you a shareholder, a consumer, or a business owner? In the next circle, place your relationship with foreign nations. What nations besides your own have you visited? Do you have friends living in or having emigrated from other parts of the world? Do you have family members served in the military in other parts of the world? Have you ever felt led to pray for another nation or people group? Finally, consider your relationship with life and death. Have you had to struggle with serious health issues? Have you recently experienced the death of a loved one?

1. Which of your relationships fan the image of God within you?
   Within which relationships are you helping to cultivate the
   image of God in others? Which ones are characterized by truth

telling, reciprocity, mutual respect, dignity, empowerment, access to resources, justice, integrity, grace, and love? Within which relationships are you compelled to say, "This is very good!" Place a circle around those relationships.

2. Now, which relationships seem to diminish the image of God in you? Within which are you neglecting to fan the image of God in other people? Which ones are characterized by lies, lack of reciprocity, disrespect, humiliation, exploitation, impoverishment, masks, shame, or fear? Which relationships compel you to say, "This is not good." Underline those relationships.

3. Pray. Thank God for the very good relationships in your life. They are like light in the darkness. They place boundaries on the pain in life. Whether they are good relationships with your family or with a local school, hospital, or branch of government, these good relationships are a blessing. Give thanks.

4. Pray again. Meditate on the relationships that have brought the most darkness into your life. Invite Creator God, Elohim, to hover over the deep (the chaos) in those relationships. Invite God to speak light, love, life, and hope into your soul concerning the relationships that bring the most pain. Invite God to be with you in the deep as you confront the sea monsters in your life. Invite God to bring clarity, to place boundaries on the pain, and to restore the image of God within you where your inherent dignity and capacity to exercise dominion have been diminished or crushed by encounters with evil.

God's intent for the world is that all aspects of creation would live in forcefully good relationship with one another. This is what "very goodness" looks like: all humanity living into its call and capacity to exercise dominion. It looks like governance that honors and stewards the image of God in every corner of the earth and stewards the rest of creation with care and protection. This is God's intent. This is what the Kingdom of God—the rule of God and governance of God—looks like. This is the very good news! But if God intended for all relationships to be forcefully good, then why are we so far from that very good world now? What happened? Why are very good relationships so rare? How do we get more of that very goodness in our relationships and world right now?

Have you heard the story of the two trees and the Fall?

Two Trees and the Fall

The first time I tried to read the book of Genesis, I was in high school and a newbie to church and faith. I wasn't very familiar with Scripture; I knew just a few verses my youth leader made us memorize, mostly in the gospel of John. So when I opened the Bible and turned to Genesis, I felt as though I had gotten in way over my head. It came across as gibberish. I mean, what's up with all the "And God said" stuff and the waters bringing forth swarms of living creatures?

Honestly, during that venture, I never made it to Genesis chapter 2. And it didn't seem as if I needed to. No sermon mentioned it, and no Bible study leader attempted to explore it. So it just sat there in the front of my Bible, helping to establish that the Bible is big, with many books, written by a lot of writers. In fact, the first time I remember cracking open my Bible to Genesis 2 was when I was on staff with a college ministry. I heard an incredible talk about Genesis 2 given by Dr. Steve Hayner, former president of the college ministry. It drove me to study the text with students on campus, and I was amazed by what we found.

Genesis 2 offers an intimate narrative of creation. This is no sweeping epic poem. Instead, we see God get down into the muck, with God's hands in the mud. God is intimately involved in the creation of humanity. This text comes from a different writer than Genesis 1. The Genesis 2 writer is known as the Yahwist, always using the name Yahweh or Yahweh Elohim for God's name. The Yahwist is also writing about four hundred years before the priests penned Genesis 1 and is making a different point.[1]

The description of this creation process begins with the words "in the day [*yom*] that the LORD God made the earth and the heavens" (Genesis 2:4), rather than in the seven days mentioned in Genesis 1. The word for "day" here can mean an actual day, from sunup to sundown, or it can mean a period of time, an age, or the days when a cited event or action took place. What is clear is that this writer didn't believe that the length of time of the creation process mattered enough to specify it.

We also can tell it's a separate narrative from that of Genesis 1 because of the discrepancy in the order of creation. In Genesis 1, humanity was the lastborn in creation. In Genesis 2, however, humanity is the first (see verse 7). Vegetation and animals were created ahead of humanity in Genesis 1 but following humanity in Genesis 2. Also, Genesis 1 begins with "the deep"; Genesis 2 begins with a mist or vapor rising from the earth. So if the point of Genesis 2 is not to provide a strictly factual account of exactly how the universe was made, then what is it? I think it's something more. I believe that the point is to teach us a higher truth about our relationships with God and one another.

In this writer's narrative, God's garden is so lush and abundant that rivers flow from it. Think of the last river you saw. I grew up in Philadelphia with the Schuylkill River running through the center of the city. Is there a river near you? Where is its origin? Rivers are made up of small streams that converge. But the four rivers in Eden spring from the garden, then separate and flow outward! That is the essence of abundance: flowing outward. This is the world God made; this is what the world is like under God's rule. It is lush.

The writer of Genesis 2 calls God *Yahweh Elohim,* which means self-existent and supreme God. In case there is any confusion over which character in the story is God and which character is not, the writer makes it clear. The human (*adam,* a word that means "human being," not "man" or "male") is made from the dust. Here in the beginning, a relationship is budding between God and humanity. God is supreme and self-existent yet personal, present, touching, connecting with, and molding humanity out of the dust. God is personally invested. And God doesn't zap humanity to life. No, God kisses us. The breath of God makes human life possible.

And God prepares a home, a garden in Eden, where God places the human. Here we get a picture of God's dominion in the form of God as an extravagant provider. This garden is not a backyard garden. By the measurements listed in verses 10–14, Eden is as big as some small countries today.

"Out of the ground the LORD God made to grow every tree that is pleasant to the sight and good for food" (verse 9). That is extravagant. God's actions reveal deep love for humanity. Only love would compel a self-existent God who can't be coerced by any higher power to pull out the stops and craft a world that is not only functional but beautiful and abundant. Love does that.

And love shares power. The Genesis 2 writer doesn't use the word *dominion* but clarifies what dominion looks like. "The LORD God took the man and put him in the garden of Eden to till it [*abad*] and keep [*shamar*] it" (verse 15). The Hebrew word for till is *abad,* which also means "to serve." The Hebrew word for keep is *shamar,* which means "to protect." Dominion—stewardship—looks like serving and protecting the rest of creation. Here the writer of Genesis 2 reveals humanity's essential calling, which is to serve and protect the needs, boundaries, and well-being of the rest of creation.

THE POWER IN NAMING

The text shows God sharing power with humanity in another way: by granting the power to name the animals. Parents name children. In many indigenous cultures, communities name adolescents as they enter adulthood. Masters name slaves. There is power in the act of naming. God places that power in the hands of humanity, but it is not given just for the sake of exercising power; it's offered in the context of relationship with God and the rest of creation and what would become the human's relationship with "bone of my bones and flesh of my flesh."

> There is power in the act of naming.

The naming process involves knowing the other deeply enough to properly see, identify, and name both the other and the self. Humanity entered into relationship with the rest of creation and discovered their names, and through that process, humanity became more acquainted with the self. The process clarified for *adam* that there was no companion of humankind to be discovered (see Genesis 2:20).

And then God made Woman! (We'll dig more deeply into this in chapter 5.) What's important here is that God saw the need for humanity to have a companion, and God came through.

Adam cried out,

This at last is bone of my bones
>   and flesh of my flesh;
this one shall be called Woman,
>   for out of Man this one was taken. (verse 23)

On our most basic level, we were created for relationship with God, within community, with the rest of creation, and between genders. And on a deeper level, all human relationships depend on one central relationship: humanity's relationship with God. After all, our life breath—life itself—was given by God. The community of the rest of creation was given by God. And, ultimately, the extravagant gift of bonded human companionship was the gift of God. What human fulfillment can there be apart from God?

THE VISION AND THE TWO TREES

What does love require? That is the question of the two trees.

In the first chapter of this book, we explored a biblical vision of shalom: what the reign of God looks like. From Genesis 1 and 2, shalom is a vision of a Kingdom that provides for all. It is a vision of abundance, of God's presence wiping away fear. It is also a vision of just and healthy interdependent relationships—a vision of respect for the image of God present in all humanity and the call and capacity of all humanity to exercise dominion. What's more, it is a vision of the self-existent, supreme God present and active in the muck with humanity. It is an intimate vision of a genuine love relationship between God and humanity, and that relationship is interconnected with all other relationships in creation.

A centerpiece of God's loving rule is revealed in the two trees mentioned in Genesis 2. We cannot understand the core nature of shalom if we do not understand the significance of the Tree of Life and the Tree of the Knowledge of Good and Evil.

God gave only one command in the garden, and it was connected to the land. The text reads, "Out of the ground the LORD God made to grow every tree that is pleasant to the sight and good for food, the tree of life also in the midst of the garden, and the tree of the knowledge of good and evil" (Genesis 2:9). A few verses later, after describing the opulence and location of the rivers that spring from Eden, the writer returns to the two trees: "And the LORD God commanded the man, 'You may freely eat of every tree of the garden; but of the tree of the knowledge of good and evil you shall not eat, for in the day that you eat of it you shall die'" (verses 16–17).

The meaning of the two trees has been debated for millennia. The Tree of Life is like the mythic fountain of youth. Humanity had to eat from only the Tree of Life to live for eternity. The Tree of the Knowledge of Good and Evil, on the other hand, has inspired a more diverse set of theories. Common lore paints the picture of an apple tree with mystical powers. Some modern interpretations speculate that the writer introduces the tree as a literary device to symbolize sexual pleasure. I'm not a fan of either of these theories.

I believe that the writer intended us to see the tree's fruit as just that: fruit. There was nothing particularly evil about it. The one distinction that makes this tree stand out is that it has a command attached to it. That command was the only boundary humanity had in paradise. It was the one place in this vast garden where humanity was confronted with the question *Do I love God?*

Before we go forward, let's pause here. It's important that we grasp the meaning of *knowledge* in order to fully understand the text. Knowledge as

we think of it in Western culture is located in the mind. To know something is to understand it intellectually. In the Hebrew culture, however,
knowledge was experiential. It was kinetic. In addition, the Hebrew word
that is used here, *da'ath,* can be translated as "awareness." The original readers would likely have understood the Tree of the Knowledge of Good and
Evil to be a tree that offered the awareness of both good *and* evil through
experience. The garden is overflowing with goodness. The humans have
had no experience of evil. The only possibility for them to have that experience exists in interaction with the Tree of the Knowledge of Good and Evil.
To eat of that tree would bring death—the ultimate separation from life,
companionship, and a community of creation bound together in an intri-
cate web of relationships. Death is the ultimate pain in a world characterized by abundant life.

God earnestly says, "Don't do it! I want you to live life to the full. I want
you and your children and your children's children to know shalom. I want
you to know my love. I want you to know a lush and lavish world, a world
where all relationships are intercon-
nected and work for the good of all,
a world without human exploitation
and slavery, without droughts, without
broken families, without domestic violence, without eating disorders, with-

> I want you to know a
> lush and lavish world, a
> world where all relation-
> ships are interconnected.

out rape, without war, without glass ceilings, ethnic enmity, and structural
racism, nationalism, and other-ism. I want you to live in a world where your
ability to exercise agency to serve and protect the rest of creation, to exercise
dominion, is unhampered by poverty or oppression. I want you to know
shalom." And what does shalom require? The cornerstone is love.

Trust and choice are two of the most basic requirements of an adult love relationship. What is a love relationship without trust? Broken. What is a love relationship without choice? At best it is an arranged marriage, but there is no guarantee that love will develop. At worst, a relationship without choice is slavery. I believe that the significance of the Tree of the Knowledge of Good and Evil in this paradise is that the tree was the only place where the humans encountered the God-craving.

Blaise Pascal said, "What else does this craving, and this helplessness, proclaim but that there was once in man a true happiness, of which all that now remains is the empty print and trace? This he tries in vain to fill with everything around him, seeking in things that are not there the help he cannot find in those that are, though none can help, since this infinite abyss can be filled only with an infinite and immutable object; in other words by God himself." I believe the God-craving was planted in the humans' hearts at the moment when God planted that tree in the garden. Humanity is tempted to fill the vacuum with all manner of things, among them sex, drugs, money, power, and success. But only one thing can fill it: relationship with God.

And so the question arises with every encounter between the humans and the tree: *Do I love God?* To love God is to trust God, to choose God, and to choose God's way to peace and wholeness. To choose the tree would be to turn our backs on God in favor of the illusion of human fulfillment apart from God.

Genesis 1 and 2 offer clear pictures of the Kingdom of God, showing what it looks like and what it requires of its citizens. God created us in an interconnected web of overwhelmingly good relationships, and love is the powerful tie that binds us together. The choices we make regarding how we gain peace reveal whether or not we trust God and choose God's ways to peace and fulfillment. To choose the Tree of the Knowledge of Good and Evil—which results in greed, consumption, exploitation, nationalism, misogyny, and other-ism—is to become an enemy of God's purposes in our world.

But what happened? When we watch the evening news, we cannot deny that humanity is far from the vision. We were created for shalom, but we are far from living in shalom.

The Fall

Genesis 3 paints the scenario that is the hinge point of history. Humanity grasps at its own peace at the expense of the peace of all. The relationships that were declared *tov me'od* in the beginning all are decimated. Here lies the wreckage of that fateful moment of original sin, the moment when humanity chose not to trust God's way to peace. Instead, humanity chose its own way. The consequences of humanity's kind of dominion—the kind of rule that governs with self-interest above the interests of the other—are sin, separation, and death.

The Greek word translated as "sin" is derived from a Greek archery term that means "to miss the mark of perfection." This word along with the ancient Greek cultural focus on the individual fundamentally shaped the modern Christian view of sin. Consequently, Christians typically seek perfection in a person's character and unblemished outward behavior. But the Hebraic concept of *tov me'od* gives us a sense of what God considers emphatically good (perfect): relational wholeness and wellness. As we saw earlier, *tov me'od* in Genesis 1 does not necessarily refer to the very goodness of the object itself; it refers to the completeness of the whole and the overwhelming wellness of the relationships among all its aggregate parts. If this is the Hebrew conception of perfection, then sin is anything that breaks the relationships that God called *tov me'od* in the beginning. Sin is (and causes) separation.

So in Genesis 3, we see the serpent sidle up to the woman and tell her God isn't worthy of her trust. "Did God say, 'You shall not eat from any tree in the garden'?" the serpent asks. The woman counters the serpent's overreach. "We may eat of the fruit of the trees in the garden," she corrects the serpent, "but God said, 'You shall not eat of the fruit of the tree that is in the middle of the garden, nor shall you touch it, or you shall die.'"

This interaction holds the first distortion of God's words. God never said, "Don't *touch* the fruit of the Tree of the Knowledge of Good and Evil"; rather, God warned not to *eat* of it. The woman did a curious thing in that she restricted her own freedom and said God had done it. Here we see the first cracks form in the relationship between humanity and God. It began with the story the woman told herself about God. Her story held some truth, but not enough to be truthful. Her story led to distrust of God, which led the humans to choose their own way to peace, fulfillment, and wholeness. For them, shalom was about knowledge, and knowledge would make them like God. So the serpent promised knowledge and told them God was trying to hold out on them. The tragedy is that they were already made in God's likeness (see Genesis 1:26).

> Love would have led the man and woman to ask God about the tree before eating from it.

Love would have led the man and woman to ask God about the tree before eating from it. Love would have led them to trust God's heart and intentions. But they didn't love God with their actions, and down went the interconnected web of relationships that God had created. The relationships were ripped apart, separated by sin.

Humanity hid from God (see Genesis 3:8–9). The husband blamed his wife, focused on his work, and ruled over her. She was left longing for the intimacy they used to know (see verses 12, 16, 19). The first animal sniped at a human being (see verse 15), and humanity had to beat the earth to get anything from it. No longer did the earth produce fruit without the investment of human labor (see verses 17–19). And death entered the world when God ripped an animal apart and skinned it to cover humanity's shame (see verse 21). Humanity was driven from the garden and separated from the Tree of Life (see verses 22–24). Brother rose up against brother, breaking families into fragments (see 4:1–16). Languages were confused and people groups were scattered (see 11:1–9), and nations declared war against the threat of imperial oppression (see 14:1–16).

The snowball of sin continues to roll forward, growing larger and destroying more of God's creation as it goes. Thirteen chapters after all relationships in creation were declared very good, nations are at war. This separation is the progeny of sin. Separation looks like distrust, shame, confusion, and domination.

But this is not the end of the story.

The rest of Scripture from Genesis to Revelation is God's restoration and redemption plan, God's plan to redeem the world and restore shalom.

What is the substance of shalom? Theologian Perry B. Yoder surveyed multiple conceptions of shalom in his book *The Meaning of Peace*. Yoder explained that shalom is both a state of being and the state of relationships. It occurs in the context of covenant relationships and is a gift from God, not something humanity can gin up. It fundamentally refers to wholeness and health and to a world in which the outcome of law is social justice. In a world characterized by shalom, God is sovereign and political treaties are part of the shalom-building process.[2]

In his book *Peace,* Walter Brueggemann wrote about the components of shalom. Brueggemann's vision includes steadfast love, faithfulness, and righteousness (see Psalm 85:10), which reside at the heart of shalom. They restore the goodness of all relationships. Brueggemann highlighted shalom's promise of well-being for all, not just individuals or segments of society (see Jeremiah 29:11–14). Finally, he reflected on Micah 5:2–5, an Advent text that promises that a leader will come from Bethlehem and will bring shalom ("social welfare, security, and well-being" in "concrete and material" ways, according to Brueggemann). He concluded, "In Christian reading it is an anticipation of Jesus."[3]

Shalom is both the antidote to sin's separation and the fruit of loving and trusting God.

IMPLICATIONS

What are the implications of this understanding of sin and shalom? Sin is not about the personal imperfection of the self. Rather, sin is any act that breaks any of the relationships God declared very good in the beginning.

As a result, the antidote to sin is not personal perfection—it is radical love! In the Sermon on the Mount, Jesus said, "You have heard that it was said, 'You shall love your neighbor and hate your enemy.' But I say to you, Love your enemies and pray for those who persecute you, so that you may be children of your Father in heaven; for he makes his sun rise on the evil and on the good, and sends rain on the righteous and on the unrighteous. . . . Be perfect, therefore, as your heavenly Father is perfect" (Matthew 5:43–45, 48). I used to think the charge to be perfect felt disconnected from all that Jesus said leading up to that statement. A more careful reading shows that being perfect as God is perfect is about radical love. Jews understood perfection to be about the quality of relationship, not individual perfection. The command to "be perfect, therefore, as your heavenly father is perfect" refers to how the Father loves perfectly. What does that look like? It looks like loving your enemy. Very goodness looks like radical love.

Reflection Exercise

Close your eyes.

Sit in silence for one minute.

Imagine your heart as a stream where the deepest longings of your soul rest like rocks beneath the surface.

Invite God to raise each rock to the surface and show you its name.

For me, the rocks read "reconciliation with family," "marriage," "reconciliation with my own body," "no more tears," and "a world where love of others characterizes our public policies." What are your rocks named?

Pray over each rock and offer the rocks back to God, the One who made the stream, who is the water, and who protects your heart.

This chapter began with a radical vision of the extravagant web of relationships God created in the beginning. We witnessed the snowball of sin rolling through time, shattering every relationship God created. Finally, we connected with our hearts' longing for shalom.

From Genesis to Revelation, the rest of Scripture is the story of God's work to redeem the very goodness of all creation and to restore shalom on earth—all through the power of radical love. That love has the power to touch and heal every corner of our lives and our world. In each chapter that follows, we will go deeper in our examination of each relationship that broke at the Fall. We'll ask, "How did the relationship break? How does that brokenness play itself out in Scripture? How does God heal?" And finally, "What does healing look like right now in real time?"

We are about to embark on a pilgrimage toward healing and restored relationships, which is nothing less than a powerful encounter with the very good gospel.

Shalom with God

Creator God. God of the universe. The beginning and the end. The One who existed before all things existed. The One who made all things. That God created us and loves us. God really loves us. That is the core premise of the gospel. The human experience knows no greater love than the love lived out in the context of marriage. It is the ultimate commitment, the joining of two to become one. Two people, two families, two sets of dreams and callings and issues and phobias and memories and jokes and cares and concerns and triumphs and lives become one, "until death do us part."

Marriage is at once beautiful, awe-inspiring, and terrifying. It is terrifying because with the deepest union comes the terror of the deepest loss. The breakup of a marriage can feel like the breaking of one's own body, soul, dreams, memories, jokes, triumphs, and even one's own life. If that is what it's like between two humans, imagine what it feels like between creation and Creator.

Our very existence depends on God. Genesis 2 tells us it is God's breath that fills our bodies. Psalm 139 tells us it was God's imagination that dreamed us into being and that God's hands formed each of us in the secret place of our mothers' wombs. God is before us. God is inside us. God surrounds us. In God we truly "live and move and have our being" (Acts 17:28). To be whole is to be in love relationship with God.

I didn't understand this growing up, but I did wonder. I'd lie on the ground and look up at the sky, wondering where God was. I would imagine God as an old man on a throne taking requests, like Santa Claus but without the red suit. I imagined angels flying to and fro around God and around the earth.

I imagined what God was like before I had ever attended a church service or opened a Bible. Something in my soul longed for God, knowing that God existed beyond what I could see. I believe that my soul was reaching for God long before I had the language that would help me understand the search. It makes me emotional still, thinking about it.

It's almost painful to go back to that space. At the same time that I was dreaming of God beyond the clouds, I also was suffering sexual abuse at the hands of a family member, bullying from schoolmates, my parents' divorce, and the loss of a beloved grandparent. I was lost and groping for an anchor.

My parents separated when I was in fifth grade. They divorced and then married other people by the start of my seventh-grade year. My mom married a well-respected man in New Jersey. We moved to Cape May to join him and his three kids, but I begged my mom to let me take the train to Philadelphia so I could still go to school there. Throughout my elementary school experience, I dreamed of going to the Philadelphia High School for Girls, the most competitive high school in the city—with the exception of Boys' High, which my grandfather had attended. Cape May was mostly

white. I had grown up in a mostly black urban area. The thought of going
to a mostly white rural school scared the bejeezus out of me.

"Please, Mom," I pleaded. "Please let me take the train to school in
Philly. Please!"

But she wouldn't back down.

The school bus would pick up my stepbrother and me, the only two
black passengers, on the shoulder of Route 9, right in front of our house. We
lived in the three-hundred-person town of Erma, New Jersey. On the first
day of school, a girl named Starla boarded about three stops later. She had
the brightest eyes and warmest smile I'd ever seen. Though she was one year
ahead of me, she sat with me. We became fast bus buddies.

I made my way in Cape May for that first year in spite of teasing from
white male classmates who joked about wanting to date me. I suffered the
humiliation of being placed in general-education classes even though I had
been in the highest reading group in a competitive class in Philadelphia. I
eventually made friends, had crushes that never went anywhere, and endured bullying.

Starla graduated from junior high school and went on to the area high
school, so my eighth-grade year was spent without her smile and her warmth.
Marching band and ecology club dulled the sting of alienation. Missing my
father and my grandparents, I filled my time mastering rifle twirling while
marching and trying to fit in with the cool kids in the ecology club.

When I think back on those days, tears flood my eyes. I was so lost.
And the thing is, part of me knew it while the other part tried to cover it up.
Like the typical teen from an eighties John Hughes movie, I wore tight
jeans, donned black eyeliner, straightened my hair, took my first sips of al-
cohol, and dreamed of the day when my crush would ask me out. He never

did, not in that southern white town. Yes, Cape May is south of the Mason-Dixon line.

The philosopher and mathematician Blaise Pascal said that the infinite abyss of our souls could be filled with only one thing: God.[1]

I chased love as if it would fill the abyss in my soul, but I had a strike against me: I was the only black person in my white, southern, semirural circle of friends. Glances turned to laughter, turned to friendship, turned to flirting, turned to friends hanging out on boardwalks, turned to bottles spun and pointing at white boys who turned tail to date "their kind." I chased love and it turned to heartbreak again and again and again. I felt as though my soul had been marked "unworthy of love."

THE SAMARITAN WOMAN

A woman approached Jacob's well at high noon in the desert outside the city of Sychar in Samaria. Most Samaritan women came to draw water in the early morning or at dusk to avoid the heat of the noonday sun. They walked together and socialized at the well in this patriarchal society. But this woman didn't. She walked alone, lugging her water jars under the high desert sun. Perhaps, being alone, she could find peace.

What was she trying to avoid? The backstory provided in John 4:16–18 explains that the woman had previously had five husbands and that the man she was with at the time was not her husband. She had given herself to five men, and five men had thrown her out. How empty must she have felt? How used? How disappointed? How unworthy of love? Five times the woman trusted a man to care and provide for her in a world in which men had multiple wives and concubines but women could have only one husband. Five times she had a home, food, and protection; five times she was thrown away. What were the chances that the man she was with at the moment would follow suit?

Perhaps this woman went to the well at noon to avoid meeting other women and enduring their whispers about her barrenness, her past worthlessness as a wife, and her conniving ways with men. Would any man see her as more than a brief pit stop?

The nameless woman approached the well. Instead of the solitude she sought, she found a Jewish man—her enemy—sitting near the well.

Verse 4 says that Jesus and his disciples had to go through Samaria on their way from Judea to Galilee, although there was an alternate route that would have taken them far out of the way. Still, Jews commonly took the longer route to avoid Samaritans. The northern kingdom of Israel had been sacked by Assyria in 722 BCE. The people were sent into exile and scattered throughout the Assyrian Empire, while Assyria brought people from conquered ethnic groups into the northern territory. Jews who had remained behind violated Mosaic Law by adopting the gods of the new inhabitants. While the Samaritans held many beliefs in common with the Jews, they maintained key differences, the most consequential of which was the Samaritans' belief that Mount Gerizim—not Jerusalem—was the land where God had commanded Moses to instruct the people to build an altar (see Deuteronomy 11:29–30). The Samaritans built a temple on Mount Gerizim and worshiped the God of Abraham there. Violent clashes took place for centuries between Jews and Samaritans. According to the Jewish historian Josephus, within Jesus's lifetime, during the year 8 CE, the Samaritans scattered human bones in the Jewish temple at Passover—an absolute abomination.[2] Since Jesus could have taken an alternate route, why did he go through Samaria? As he approached the city of Sychar, the disciples split off to go buy food, but Jesus sat by Jacob's well under the high desert sun.

The gospel writer John mentioned Jacob's name three times. The original hearers would have recalled the significance of the well in the lives of several patriarchs. A well serves as a metaphor for a place of legacy and love. It is a place where deals are made and people are set apart for God's purposes.[3] Jesus sat by Jacob's well, and the nameless Samaritan woman—representing a cross section of ethnicities and living on the margin of the margins—met him there. Jesus opened a conversation with four words: "Give me a drink" (John 4:7). This echoes a story told in Genesis 24. Abraham sent his servant to find a wife for Abraham's son Isaac. The servant completed his task at a well. Rebekah walked up, and the first thing the servant said to her was, "Give me a drink." Rebekah later became Isaac's wife.

Likewise, when Jesus asked the Samaritan woman to give him a drink, he was setting the stage for a marriage. Just prior to this, Jesus had said to his disciples, "He who has the bride is the bridegroom" (3:29). John's gospel raises the question, Who is the bride and who is the bridegroom? In John 4:7, Jesus answered the question with four words: "Give me a drink." Jesus is the bridegroom. As Jesus waited at a well and asked for a drink of water, the God of all creation crossed space and time to propose to humanity! And in asking this of a Samaritan woman, Jesus showed that God's love is not limited by ethnicity, gender, or social status.

I love the woman's sassy comeback: "How is it that you, a Jew, ask a drink of me, a woman of Samaria?" (verse 9). In other words, "You can't be for real. You can't want to be with me, because no one wants to be with me, and least of all you Jews!"

Jesus answered her, "If you knew the gift of God, and who it is that is saying to you, 'Give me a drink,' you would have asked him, and he would have given you living water" (verse 10). Jesus explained that the water he was offering would never run out. His living water gushes up to eternal life, and those who drink it never thirst again.

God speaks of living water in the book of Jeremiah. Yahweh pleads with his harlot wife, Israel:

I remember the devotion of your youth,
 your love as a bride,
how you followed me in the wilderness,
 in a land not sown.
Israel was holy to the LORD. . . .

What wrong did your ancestors find in me
 that they went far from me
and went after worthless things, and became worthless
  themselves? . . .

Be appalled, O heavens, at this,
 be shocked . . .
for my people have committed two evils;
 they have forsaken me,
the fountain of living water,
 and dug out cisterns for themselves,
cracked cisterns
 that can hold no water. (2:2–3, 5, 12–13)

God had said to the Israelites some seven hundred years earlier, "You were devoted to me as a loving bride. You loved me. You followed me. But now you drink from cups that can hold no water. You are thirsty."

Humanity is thirsty for God, but we drink from cups that can hold no water. We draw well water and find that we are thirstier after we drink our fill. It is the water of self-hatred and rejection. It is the water of shame, isolation, and chemical dependence. It is the water of misogyny and patriarchy. It is the water of toxic dumping and climate change. It is the water of violence and neglect, the water of nationalism. Well water throws you into depression, rage, self-pity, isolation, and narcissism. The best that well water can offer is momentary bliss followed by hell on earth.

But Jesus reminded the Samaritan woman that she was created for living water. The woman who had repeatedly been rejected was created for water that brings God's healing, acceptance, and wholeness. She was created for Gods' peace between ethnic groups and genders. She was created for places where living water springs from the earth and waters everything and everyone in its path. This hardened woman was created to be loved and to love.

I have come to believe that the journey of our lives from birth to death is a journey back to God. Psalm 139 says God knit us together in our mothers' wombs, but that is the stuff of sinew and bone. What of spirit and soul? The prophet opened his book with this word from God: "Before I formed you in the womb I knew you" (Jeremiah 1:5). Before we had bodies, we were with God and known by God, and (I imagine) we knew God. God is our home, and from birth to death, the whole of our lives is a journey to return home.

Genesis 2 offers the first glimpse of living water. It gushes up from the Garden of Eden and spreads across the earth in four directions. It creates lush living space, safety, and fruitful work. Then comes the break. *Ish* and *ishsha* choose their own way to peace rather than God's way. They trust the serpent rather than the words of God. God later enters the garden looking for beloved humanity. The man and woman hide, unsure of God's intention toward them. The break is taking its toll. Within sixteen verses shalom is ransacked, with every relationship that had been declared *tov me'od* now broken.

Humanity's broken relationship with God is the ultimate cause of all other brokenness. In another sense, there is no way humanity could violate relationship with any other created being and not violate its relationship with God. Creation is bound together by relationship with our Creator since it is Creator God's love that binds us together. To break one tie is to break them all.

> The whole of our lives is a journey to return home.

The first humans were tempted to grasp for their own way to peace in the garden, but their futile reach left them emptier than when they began. They reached for peace and received the empty promise of well water. At the start of his ministry, Jesus was tempted in the desert (see Luke 4:1–13). He wrestled against the temptation to fill his own hunger, to usurp power, and to doubt God's capacity to give life. In the end, Jesus chose God's way to peace, and the reversal of the Fall began.

As Jesus sat at the well talking with the woman, he spoke not only to her heart but also to her mind. She had real concerns about the rightful place of worship—concerns hewn out of centuries of ethnic strife. Jesus honored her by engaging her questions.

WE ARE STILL ASKING JESUS QUESTIONS

I had so many questions myself. I wanted to know, Who is God? What is prayer? Who is Jesus, and why do people talk about him as if he's still alive?

At the same time, the God-shaped abyss in my soul was hungry to be filled. Born black in a white world, a woman in a man's world, I became a child survivor of bullying, sexual abuse, and divorce. I was lost and trying my best to be okay.

When I graduated from junior high and started riding the high school bus, Starla, the girl with the bright smile, was there again. She invited me to sit with her on my first day of high school. Soon after, I was invited by another friend to attend a meeting of an area-wide youth group. Kids called it Y, but I never knew if it was Y or Why. Either way worked for me. (I now think it was Y, short for Young Life, a national ministry for high school students.)

I went to the meeting and Starla was there. She welcomed me, and her friends welcomed me, and other kids (some cool, some not so cool) all welcomed me. It was a first for me. I felt welcomed before I ever did a thing to earn it. I asked tons of questions over the course of the next year. My love for God grew as I became part of this community that served as a small haven through its ministry of welcome.

Toward the end of the summer of 1983, I started a diet, one of several I had tried. My battle against the temptation to use ice cream and cake for comfort began with my parents' divorce and our move from Philadelphia to Cape May in 1980. I stepped on the scale the morning of August 21, 1983, and logged my weight.

I had been asking questions about God and Jesus and prayer for nearly a year. I started visiting the small country church that Starla was part of. Her dad and mom (the pastor and youth leader, respectively), her friends (the youth group), her brother, and one or two senior citizens walked with me through my year of questions. Then, on August 21, 1983, Starla's dad was away on vacation. He had told the congregation to worship at the Sunday evening camp church meeting where a guest preacher was headlining a revival meeting.

Surrounded by woods and ticks, the guest preacher took the stage just off a two-lane country road in Erma, New Jersey. The church youth group sat in a middle row toward the back of the wooden pavilion. The preacher screamed about hell for what felt like forever. Then as the organ played, he invited the lost to come to the front and get right with God by accepting Jesus Christ as personal Lord and Savior. He urged us not to wait another minute.

I remembered all the things I'd done for God over the past year. There were walk-a-thons for Jesus and sing-a-thons for Jesus. I played my flute at church and abstained from drinking at the school musical's cast party. Plus, I didn't curse anymore. That had to count for something. I wasn't sure if I was a Christian. When could I stop wondering during every altar call if I should walk forward?

In the middle of my mental gymnastics, a friend tapped me on the shoulder and asked if I would go forward with her. To this day, I don't understand why she felt the need to go forward. I thought she was already a Christian. I went with her and we knelt at the altar, where she wept openly. Soon I felt sobs well up from somewhere deep in my own soul. It was as if something in my spirit had thrown up its hands and said to God, *Okay, you win. I'm not going to fight anymore. I give up.* It was a giving up of control over my life and fate, a giving up of the need to earn my own way to heaven. Then it was even more. As I sobbed alongside my friend, we were surrounded by old ladies who comforted us. It was a strange feeling, like a spiritual homecoming. It was as though the old souls were ushering younger ones across a threshold to a spiritual place called home. What happened in me that night was about power and love. As tears fell on the wooden altar, I felt like I was surrounded by the heart of God. I knew, finally, that God loved me.

While the preacher had focused on hell, I've come to understand that God's work in me that night was less about salvation from hell in an afterlife, though I do believe in the reality of hell. Rather, that night was about the power of Jesus's resurrection from the dead to reverse the Fall here on earth *and* in the afterlife.

> As tears fell on the wooden altar, I felt like I was surrounded by the heart of God.

Humanity was driven from the garden in Genesis 3. The man and woman were kept from finding the Tree of Life, for fear they would eat of it and live forever under deteriorating circumstances. Thus, death entered the world and separated humanity from life itself, from each other, and from God. Separation is the consequence of sin. As we discussed earlier, sin is anything that breaks any relationship that God declared "very good." Death is the ultimate form of separation. In Genesis 3, death won, sin won, and separation won.

But the story was not over. Jesus died, was placed in the grave, descended into hell, unlocked the gates of hell, and beat death! Overcome with the implications of Jesus's resurrection, Paul broke into song in his first letter to the Corinthian church: "Death has been swallowed up in victory. Where, O death, is your victory? Where, O death, is your sting?" (1 Corinthians 15:54–55). In Christ, sin no longer has the victory. Separation no longer has the victory. Jesus beat death, so we are no longer slaves to it. We are no longer slaves to separation.

In his second letter to the Corinthians, Paul wrote, "If anyone is in

Christ, there is a new creation: everything old has passed away; see, everything has become new!" (5:17). The Greek word for creation (*kitisis*) in this text means "the *act of* creation." Here's another way to read it: "If anyone is in Christ, there is a new *act of* creation." When each person reenters a love relationship with God, a new act of creation is taking place. God is recreating the world one person at a time.

On that late summer night, I rose from the altar and was overcome by a wave of laughter. I felt giddy and new, as if a light had been turned on in my soul. It was as if I had awakened after a lifelong haze of half sleep, half life. I could feel it, though I didn't have the language for it yet. I felt the power of the Resurrection. As my friends drove me home, I remember thinking, *I wonder if I'll still be a Christian ten years from now.* That was 1983.

Until the end of the American Civil War, slaves were not permitted to legally marry. So rather than conducting a typical marriage ceremony, men and women who vowed to love, serve, and protect each other till death, the master's whip, or their sale made them part signified their commitment by jumping over a handcrafted broom. On one side of the broom, they were single; on the other, the two became one in the spiritual realm. I've come to refer to the night I walked down the aisle at the church camp meeting as the night I jumped the broom with Jesus. That night Jesus said, "I love you, Lisa. You *are* worth pursuing. I have pursued you across two thousand years. I broke the barriers of time and space to be with you again." That night I said yes to Jesus. I dropped my well water at the altar, and Jesus's living water began to trickle up from my soul.

I weighed myself when I got home that night, and I was ten pounds lighter. I believe those ten pounds were real. I had been carrying a spiritual weight so oppressive it had registered on the scale.

My problems, issues, and brokenness weren't all taken away that night.

But something real—something transformative—had happened at the altar. I entered back into relationship with God through the person of Jesus. In the decades since August 21, 1983, God has revealed the presence and impact of broken relationships in my life. God revealed a deep sense of self-hatred and shame as well as broken relationships with men that stemmed from childhood abuse. God revealed a penchant toward overconsumption and a disregard for the rest of creation. God revealed hopelessness for the healing of my fractured family as well as the reality of my social, economic, and political status as an African American in the United States and within the evangelical church. God also revealed my American privilege on the global stage.

> I had been carrying a spiritual weight so oppressive it had registered on the scale.

The revelations came slowly as I was able to handle them and with guidance from others who had trod the paths before me. In the chapters that follow, I will share some of what God has shown me on this journey. With each revelation, God has given me light, healing, and redemption. The healing has come in God's way, in God's time. And thirty-two years later, I am still waiting on God for some of the most stubborn brokenness in my soul and life to be healed. Meanwhile, I partner with God to bring healing to some of the most broken corners of our society and world.

The nameless Samaritan woman dropped her jar of well water and went back to the city to talk to the people she had tried to avoid. But something was different now. She was bold, confident, and actively loving the people who had shamed her. With no concern for what they thought of her, the woman told them about her encounter with Jesus. The text tells us, "Many Samaritans from that city believed in him because of the woman's testimony" (John 4:39). This shamed, rejected, marginalized, ethnic enemy became the first person in John's gospel to communicate the very good news and bring transformation to an entire city. The Samaritan woman and her city were transformed by God's love and power.

Reflection Exercise

Consider God's invitation: "Give me a drink." Do you believe God crosses barriers to love you and to be with you? Have you said yes to God? If so, when? If not, what holds you back?

Consider the interconnectedness of relationship with God and all relationships in creation. Do you sense God's movement in your life and soul to bring healing to others?

Consider the Resurrection. Where do you sense that God wants to speak life into your soul, your life, or your relationships? Where do you feel God's challenge to believe in the power of the Resurrection to beat death and bring new life to relationships between ethnic groups and nations?

Finally, for this exercise, fill a cup with water and consider the biblical image of well water. Imagine that the water in your cup is well water. What does the well water in your cup represent? In what areas of your life are you drinking water that leaves you thirstier than you were before you drank it?

Now consider the image of living water. What might it look like to replace your well water with God's living water?

If you're ready, dump out your well water. Let it go. Close your eyes and hold your empty cup in front of you. Say this simple prayer: "Fill me."

Shalom with Self

I was in fifth grade when one morning I came down to breakfast and my mommy told me, "Your daddy moved out last night. He loves you and he will always be your daddy." I asked why, but there was no answer good enough. I lowered my head and wept, and I felt my self-worth drain from my being. The message that replaced it was *I am not worthy of being loved*.

Researcher and storyteller Dr. Brené Brown has spent her career studying shame, vulnerability, and wholeheartedness. In her book *Daring Greatly*, she describes shame as "the fear of disconnection" and "real pain." Brown's research confirms the heart of the concept of shalom—we all are connected. We were created for connection. According to Brown, there is a direct correlation between our fear of being disconnected from one another and our level of shame. At its heart, shame is a fear that our failures, our shortcomings, our true selves make us unworthy of connection. The core lie of shame is *I am not enough*.

Brown says that the pain of shame is real. She cites research by the National Institute of Mental Health and the National Institute on Drug Abuse.

The research found that "as far as the brain is concerned, physical pain and intense experiences of social rejection hurt in the same way."[1]

The words *guilt, shame, humiliation,* and *embarrassment* are often used interchangeably. Psychologist and researcher John Bradshaw divides shame into two subcategories: healthy shame and toxic shame. Bradshaw places embarrassment, shyness, and recognition of our need for community under the category of healthy shame. He identifies toxic shame as the source of self-isolation and alienation. Toxic shame, according to Bradshaw, "is experienced as the all pervasive sense that I am flawed and defective as a human being."[2] It moves from being an emotion to becoming a core identity. Brown simply calls this shame and draws a hard line between it and guilt, humiliation, and embarrassment. The difference, she says, is the question of identity. In each case—embarrassment, humiliation, and guilt—the person experiences the emotions based on actions of self or others, but the emotions are not internalized as one's core identity.[3]

Isn't that true? Shame whispers lies into our souls about who we are in our spirits. It immobilizes us with fear of exposure. It causes us to retreat further into ourselves or strike out against the perceived accusers. In the end, we remain unknown and disconnected.

"Over the past two decades," Holly VanScoy, PhD, explains, "psychologists, psychiatrists and other mental health professionals have reported that abnormal styles of handling shame play an important role in social phobias, eating disorders, domestic violence, substance abuse, road rage, schoolyard and workplace rampages, sexual offenses and a host of other personal and social problems."[4]

Shame is insidious. It hits at the core of our being and emanates from there to affect everything else. It has nothing to do with the truth. It is based

I am loved and God loves me.

on lies about the essence of our being. We have taken in these lies from too many voices to count: parents, siblings, childhood classmates, teachers, television, film, magazines, music videos, public policies, laws, and structures. The voices have driven lies deep into the pits of our souls and drowned out the voice of the One who created us. The voice of the One who says, "I love you."

We see shame at work in Genesis 3. At the end of Genesis 2, the man and woman are "both naked, and were not ashamed." Then they listen to the serpent's lie as he tells them that if they eat the fruit of the Tree of the Knowledge of Good and Evil, they will not die. The fundamental lie is this: God lied to you. And even deeper, the lie that God does not have your best interests at heart. And the lie that goes the deepest: God doesn't love you.

The serpent continues, "For God knows that when you eat of it your eyes will be opened, and you will be like God, knowing good and evil" (3:5). According to the serpent, God is not trustworthy, so we must follow our own words, our own wants, our own ways to peace.

The man and woman eat the fruit. They trust their own way to peace. They choose not to trust God's love for them, and what is the impact? The lie burrows more deeply: "You are unlovable as you are." This is shame.

The man and woman cover their nakedness with fig leaves, a profound act that reveals they sense something is wrong with the fact that they are naked. They have introduced the first barrier between them. The fig leaves serve as a shield, as protection against disconnection.

Not only do the fig leaves serve as self-protection, they also place a barrier between the man and woman. In her research, Brown found that people said vulnerability was "like being naked."[5] In Genesis 3, we see the man and woman covering their nakedness. Shame breaks vulnerability and it is devastating. "Vulnerability," Brown explains, "is the birthplace of love, belonging, joy, courage, empathy, and creativity. It is the source of hope, empathy, accountability and authenticity."[6]

Human shame also drives a wedge between humanity and the rest of creation. To cover our shame, God gutted and skinned an animal (see verse 21). Shame breaks relationships that God declared "very good" in the beginning, prior to the first blood sacrifice.

Shame is a counteroffer to the love of God, which is the connection between all things. What exactly is this counteroffer, and how do we reject it so we are free to return to love?

SHAME'S COUNTEROFFER

Every time the first woman and man encountered the Tree of the Knowledge of Good and Evil—the tree upon which God placed the command not to eat of it—they faced a choice. They had to decide if they did in fact trust God. Will we choose God and God's ways, or will we choose our own way to peace? As I shared earlier in this book, to love God is to trust God and to choose God as well as to choose God's way to peace and wholeness. It's as if God placed the tree in the middle of the garden, in a space where the man and woman would have to encounter it. And each time they passed the tree, they had the opportunity to trust and choose God.

In the beginning, God declared all of creation to be very good (*tov me'od*). As we have discussed, the writers of Genesis were speaking not only of the separate parts of creation but also of the connections between things. If God declares that overwhelming goodness looks like the abundant wellness of all relationships, then sin is anything that breaks relationships. The counteroffer is sin, which brings separation, distrust of God, and a reliance on human protection rather than dependence on God.

Shalom says we all are connected. Every relationship created by God is strung together in a web of intimate relationships. To affect one is to affect all. So when our distrust of God leads us to separate ourselves from God, we also are separated from ourselves. We govern ourselves in our own ways, not in God's way. We don't trust ourselves. We don't choose ourselves. Even the narcissist, who seems to choose only himself, does it because of his fear that his inherent unworthiness will be exposed. He places the barrier of the appearance of perfection between himself and everyone else as protection from exposure.[7]

> Every relationship created by God is strung together in a web of intimate relationships.

That is the picture of shame, and this is its outcome. God blasted Israel for depending on Egypt for their protection rather than on their Creator:

Oh, rebellious children, says the LORD,
who carry out a plan, but not mine;
who make an alliance, but against my will,
    adding sin to sin;
who set out to go down to Egypt
    without asking for my counsel,
to take refuge in the protection of Pharaoh,
    and to seek shelter in the shadow of Egypt. (Isaiah 30:1–2)

On a national scale, the people of Israel did the same thing the man and woman did in the Garden of Eden. The people were choosing their own way to peace. It's not only that they sought an alliance with Egypt; it's that they did not consult first with God. They sought protection from a foreign power without even seeking God's protection. Through their actions they demonstrated that they trusted human means of protection more than they trusted God's means of protection.

This was the outcome: "Therefore the protection of Pharaoh shall become your shame, and the shelter in the shadow of Egypt your humiliation" (verse 3). They chose to follow their own way to peace, and their sin led to their shame.

It's not clear from the text what led the Israelites to seek shelter with Egypt. What is clear is the result of their choice:

> Because you reject this word,
>> and put your trust in oppression and deceit,
>> and rely on them;
> therefore this iniquity shall become for you
>> like a break in a high wall, bulging out, and about to collapse,
>> whose crash comes suddenly, in an instant;
> its breaking is like that of a potter's vessel
>> that is smashed so ruthlessly
> that among its fragments not a sherd is found
>> for taking fire from the hearth,
>> or dipping water out of the cistern. (verses 12–14)

Have you ever done something and later realized that your actions broke relationships? Or maybe you're a leader—a legislator, judge, pastor—and your governance helped break the relationship between the people you lead or the system itself. Or let's go even deeper. How about the things you did to break relationship with yourself through the ways you chose to govern your life poorly—your finances, your body, your mind, your mental and emotional health, and your spirit? Often the actions that break our relationships rise from our shame, our sense of unworthiness. In our attempts to cover over our nakedness, we pull back from the ones who love us, leaders distance themselves from the ones they lead. We hide, refusing to get help, and people get hurt.

And there is the sin committed against us. For instance, it's the sin of a father who disengages from the life of his son or daughter. It is the sin of a sibling who cuts his sister out of his life. It is the sin of a friend, classmate, or colleague who seeks her own interests at the expense of the other. It is the sin of a teacher who disengages from responsibility to educate the kids at the back of the room. It is the sin of a mayor who disengages from responsibility to steward whole swaths of a city. It is the sin of a legislator who disengages from responsibility to serve and protect whole people groups within a state or nation. These actions communicate lies to the souls of the brokenhearted about who they are, what they are capable of, and their value. It heaps shame on the shoulders of people who have done no wrong and has the capacity to crush souls as it declares, "You are unworthy."

In the end, shame leaves us standing alone—separated from one another. It causes us to lash out, then tells us to cover our sin, to deny it and defend it and spin it. And on the flip side, shame leads us to craft armor to protect our hearts from more disengagement and separation. This is what it looks like to sew a protective covering of fig leaves, to believe the foundational lie that this sin, ours or theirs, is confirmation that we are, indeed, worth nothing behind the fig leaves.

Returning to Love

How do we return to love? Brené Brown's teaching on wholehearted living and vulnerability is helpful. The wholehearted approach life from the position of one who is fundamentally worthy. She says, "The Wholehearted identify vulnerability as the catalyst for courage, compassion, and connection."[8]

Resistance to shame is a losing battle. As long as we care about connection, Brown says, "the fear of disconnection will always be a powerful force in our lives, and the pain caused by shame will always be real." She says the counter to shame is shame resilience—the process of moving from shame (disconnection) to empathy (connection). "If we can share our story with someone who responds with empathy and understanding, shame can't survive." Notice: The counter to shame is not self-confidence! According to Brown, "Shame is a social concept—it happens between people—it also heals best between people."

Brown recommends four practices to strengthen shame resilience:[9]

1. *Recognizing shame and understanding the triggers.* Be aware when shame is rearing its head. Take stock when you feel yourself reaching for a fig leaf. And figure out what triggered it.

2. *Practicing critical awareness.* I call it recognizing and naming the lie we're tempted to believe about ourselves. Name it out loud if you have to.

3. *Reaching out.* Share your story with an empathetic and understanding friend. Someone who has earned your trust.

4. *Speaking shame.* Shame loves secrets. It doesn't want to be named because it knows that once it is spoken, it goes poof. Voice is to shame like water is to the Wicked Witch of the West in *The Wizard of Oz*. So talk about it, and ask for what you need when you feel it.

WE ARE WORTHY

In Psalm 139, we read that God knows us and still calls us beloved. God knows our thoughts and still holds on to the same divine dream for our lives, unchanged since we were created. Even with all of our weaknesses, God doesn't run from us. Because of God's nearness, we are never alone. And why does David write that such knowledge is too wonderful for him? He was the king of Israel, but consider what David was.

He was an unlikely leader, not the one others would have chosen. He was a confessed adulterer. He was a rapist and a confessed murderer. He had multiple wives, a far cry from the picture of shalom painted in the garden. Yet God still called him and chose him and even called him a man after God's own heart.

I understand how David could struggle to believe that God smiled whenever God thought of him. I used to struggle to believe this about myself.

In grade school I was picked on by a bully who was known as Fat Alice. She sat behind me in second grade at Saint Athanasius School, across the street and a few doors down from my house in Philadelphia. Fat Alice's two goons—yes, second-grade goons—sat on either side of her. One day I was sitting at my desk, trying to focus on what the teacher was trying to teach. I kept feeling punches in my back. First on the right side (pause), then on the left (pause). The teacher chose that moment to call on me. I answered correctly.

Another punch came to my right torso. I couldn't get away. Fat Alice made me pay her twenty-five cents every day so she would be my friend. I started asking my mom for an extra quarter every day, and she gave it to me. When we got to class, I would sit at my desk and cautiously hand Fat Alice her quarter. That went on for a few days without incident.

Then one day after the last bell rang and the children left the school yard, Fat Alice and her goons shoved me right in front of a crossing guard, who did nothing. Kids called, "Fight! Fight!" There was no fight. There was only me getting beat up just feet from my home. Fat Alice's goons pulled my jacket. She punched me. I tried to get away. Kids surrounded us. I don't remember how it ended. I remember only the shame of it. I thought there must be something wrong with me. I wanted protection, in the same way the man and woman sought protection by sewing together fig leaves.

Some kids develop tough emotional shells, others work on being funny, and others feign indifference as their forms of protection from the Fat Alices of the world. These are all fig leaves. But I wasn't good at faking it. I was scared and I kept getting beat up. A belief about myself sank deeper and deeper each time. I was convinced I was helpless.

A few years later, in fifth grade, my best friend and my worst enemy teamed up. They got the entire fifth grade class to gang up on me when the teacher left the room. The boy who had asked me to be his girlfriend one year before stood over me and shouted, "Look at her big butt!" Today I look at pictures of myself from that year and I'm amazed. I wasn't fat at all. I was just an average-sized fifth grader. But that is when my overeating began. That is when I broke relationship with my body and began to use food to cover my shame.

Flash forward twenty years. I'm having trouble at work. I'm seen as combative in staff meetings. I often feel threatened, attacked, and undermined by coworkers. I strike back verbally or put up walls of silence. And after meditating on Psalm 100:1–5, I realize it doesn't make me feel good to be a sheep of God's pasture. I don't trust the other sheep!

Later that year, I attend a conference where I feel led to go to a room set aside to receive healing prayer. This type of prayer leverages the power of what Walter Brueggemann has called the prophetic imagination.[10] It is prayer that doesn't just talk to God but makes space for God to talk back through words, images, and memories. Healing prayer invites God to come in close to heal deep wounds from our pasts by identifying the lies we have believed about ourselves, about God, and about others—and to replace the lies with truth.[11]

I didn't know what I needed prayer for; I just felt led to walk into the room. It was a typical small conference room—beige everywhere. A few sets of chairs with metal legs and slightly cushioned seats were set up in circles. Three older women were there and they welcomed me.

The one who seemed to be the leader invited me to sit in one of the circles. She sat directly across from me, and the other two sat on either side. It brought to mind the seating arrangement with Fat Alice and her two goons. But this leader took my hands—both of them. She closed her eyes and invited Jesus to speak to us all, to show us what he wanted to heal. The women prayed, thanking God for bringing me to the room. They used words such as *beautiful* to describe me and affirmed God's calling on my life. Then we sat in silence and waited for God to speak.

Eventually, the leader raised her head and asked everyone if we heard anything. A few people said they felt deep pain and knew that God wanted to heal it. Then the leader shared that she saw a word. That word was written on a piece of paper and fixed to my forehead. The word was *unwanted*.

I wept.

That's it. All these years from second grade, through fifth grade, through my father's leaving us, and through every moment since, that is the core lie I've believed: I am not wanted. I am fundamentally unloved.

The leader looked into my eyes and said, "God wants to remove that label from your forehead and replace it with a new name."

We returned to prayer. The leader asked Jesus to reveal the label to me, and I saw it clearly. It was handwritten: *Unwanted.* Then the leader asked Jesus to replace the label with my new name. In my mind, I could see Jesus as he removed the old label. Then he placed a new one over my head. It read, *Wanted.*

I wept again and giggled. I couldn't stop giggling. It was the first time in more than twenty years that love had broken through. It might have been the first time ever. With my new name, my armor came down and I was free to love and be loved.

Later that year, in a time of prayer with a friend, we got a sense that God wanted to go deeper. We asked Jesus what it was that he wanted to show us. I saw my head resting on the kitchen table the morning after my daddy left us. Jesus showed me a thermometer. The mercury was dropping as I cried. That was how I felt about my worth in that moment. It dropped to half. If my daddy didn't love me enough to stay, then I was not worth very much. That lie was lodged in my heart, and I had been living with it ever since.

My friend laid her hand on my shoulder and asked Jesus to fill me with the truth of his love for me. The truth of my worth as God sees it. What God declares truth is true indeed.

I watched in my imagination as the mercury rose to full. To this day, when I am tempted to believe the lie of shame, I remember that thermometer rising to full.

Over the next several years, God revealed several other areas where shame had caused me to place fig leaves of protection over my true self. I confronted my fear of my natural black hair and what "going natural" would do to my standing in my mostly white and Asian community. I confronted my shame over debt and opened myself to a process that gave tools to achieve economic health. And I confronted the impacts of childhood sexual abuse on my ability to choose vulnerability with men.

Perhaps that was what struck David in the middle of Psalm 139. With all his weaknesses and sin, with all the pain he had caused and all that had been done to him, still God called him wanted. God called him worthy. God called him beloved.

This is very good news indeed.

 Reflection Exercise

1. Imagine a time you felt ashamed. What was the feeling like physically and emotionally?
2. Pray. Ask God to reveal the lie that shame told you about yourself and the related lie that you are unworthy of connection.
3. Take a moment to write down the lie.
4. How did you respond to the lie that was told to you? Did you reach for a fig leaf? How did you distance yourself from others or from your true self? Did you withdraw? Did you lash out? Did you seek to please or appease others?
5. If shame caused you to withdraw, lash out, or appease, ask God to show you how your response affected those around you. Take responsibility. Confess the ways your shame led you to break relationship with others. Ask for God's forgiveness.
6. Ask God to show you how God sees you.

7. Ask God to show you what living according to that truth will look like in the way you will now interact with others. Take a moment to write down what you hear.

8. Tell your story to a trusted friend, and ask your friend to pray with you. Together, pray for God to grow your shame resilience and thank God for the truth that you are loved, you are wanted, and you are enough.

Shalom Between Genders

I served as worship team leader for weekly chapter meetings in a conservative evangelical college ministry from my sophomore to senior year at Rutgers University. One night, just before the meeting, a new male staff worker took me aside and gently explained, "I'm here now, and I can play guitar and lead worship. As a woman, it's time for you to learn how to follow." I didn't understand and questioned him. I had led worship for chapter meetings for three years. But he insisted that I needed to follow him. Tears trickled down my face as I sang backup that night . . . and for the rest of my senior year, because I'm a woman.

That was my first direct, personal encounter with the theology of male dominance. It is rooted in a stream of Christian theology that declares that God's good intention for women is that they serve and follow men.

Patriarchal interpretations of Scripture fail to start at the beginning. They start after the Fall, in Genesis 3. As a result, they present observations of a fallen world as if the current state is in line with God's good intentions. That is far from the truth.

What God called very good was *before* the Fall!

The doctrine of the image of God, established in Genesis 1:26–27, has profound implications on the relationship between men and women. As we saw in chapter 2, God created humanity and declared that all humans, male and female, are created in God's image. We all are representative figures of God. In the same breath, God said, "And let them have dominion" (verse 26). The text makes no distinction between the kind of dominion that males and females are called to exercise. There is only the call to exercise co-dominion, to steward the earth, to protect and serve the rest of creation together.

Genesis 2 gives us a more detailed picture of what co-dominion looks like. In God's mercy, God said, "It is not good that the man [*adam*] should be alone; I will make him a helper [*ezer*] as his partner." *Adam* is not the man's name. It is the Hebrew word for human being, not man or male. The text tells us that rather than creating a man first, God created a human being who, in the beginning, had no distinct gender.

God saw this gender-neutral human's need for companionship and provided the answer to that need. The word God used is *ezer*, which is Hebrew for "aid; help." *Ezer* appears twenty-one times in only two contexts throughout Scripture. First, it describes the kind of help God gives to people of faith. Second, it is a military term that means the point person in a V formation, the one out in front protecting the rest. Thus, contrary to popular belief, females were not taken from the rib of a male. And they were not created as the weaker sex. In fact, the picture is much more profound.

In light of the meaning of *ezer*, we understand that either (a) the woman was created as a superior help to protect the man, in the same way that God protects humanity and a military *ezer* protects the battalion, or (b) humanity is no longer alone. Humanity now has human companionship, with each ordained to be the protector of the other. Hubris tempts me to believe that women are the superior help, but I believe the writer's intent was the latter.[1]

Second, God caused the human to fall into a deep sleep. As in Genesis 1, God separated one from the other. This time God separated male from female. God took a rib from *adam*, the human, and for the first time in the text, gender-specific language describes humanity. We see for the first time female (*ishsha*) and male (*ish*). The first human community is created, and humanity gains companionship of like kind. The human is so overcome with passion and gratitude that only poetry, not science or modern history, can communicate the depth of joy and gratitude:

> This at last is bone of my bones
> > and flesh of my flesh;
> this one shall be called Woman,
> > for out of Man this one was taken. (Genesis 2:23)

Some commentators use this passage as evidence of Adam's superior position over the woman because he named her. In her analysis of Genesis 2–3, Phyllis Trible points out that Adam did not name Eve but simply called her woman. As a result, he did not exercise power over her as he did the animals. Rather, he recognized her gender and his own gender and affirmed both in the same breath. Thus, "female and male are equal sexes," Trible wrote. "Neither has authority over the other."[2]

Finally, as Genesis 2 draws to a close, the man and woman are naked and unashamed. There is vulnerability between them. There is trust and no shame. They have chosen each other and there is acceptance. And in light of the words of the writer, who explains that this is why a man leaves his father and mother and clings to his wife, there is a deep sense of interdependence. There is shalom between them.

THE FALL

Then came the Fall. All the relationships that God called "very good" came crashing down at the Fall. The man and woman chose their own way to peace, wholeness, and wellness. The result was they reaped the only thing a human kind of peace can offer—broken peace. Immediately the blame game ensued. Fingers pointed and the break was made manifest.

The cornerstone of patriarchal biblical interpretation is right here.

Commentators who advocate biblical patriarchy make one or a combination of the following arguments:

1. Eve was gullible or pushy. God gave the command to Adam, not to Eve. She should have let Adam take the lead. Instead, she led the man astray.
2. God cursed the woman for leading her husband into sin.
3. God established the order of gender hierarchy with the declaration "Your desire shall be for your husband, and he shall rule over you" (Genesis 3:16).

On the first point, God did not give the command to a guy named Adam. God gave the command to a human being who comprised both male and female. So in essence, God gave the command to both of them. Most important, they were both present when the serpent connived. If the woman was gullible, so was the man. As the text says, he "was with her, and he ate" (verse 6).

On the second point, God never cursed the woman or the man. Rather, the rest of creation was cursed (see verses 14, 17) as a result of humanity's sin. This is a graphic demonstration of the concept of shalom—all of creation is interconnected in a web of interdependent relationships. It's like a spider web; you can't destroy one part of the web without affecting the whole.

On the third point, God's declaration to the woman that her husband will rule over her is either prescriptive or descriptive. Either God prescribes gender-based hierarchy because it is what God wants, or God describes the hierarchy that comes as a natural result of the break in relationship. To say this is what God wants is to discount all that came before. That includes the co-dominion that is stated by God in Genesis 1, and it includes gender-neutral humanity's being offered companionship through the separation of male and female from the one being in Genesis 2. Male dominance is nowhere to be found in the heart of God's intentions for humanity prior to the Fall. It makes sense that God is simply describing the natural outcome of humanity's having broken the way to peace. Humanity chose the way of dominance. Between men and women, it takes the form of patriarchy, which shows what it looks like to live in broken shalom.

THE WRECKAGE

The broken relationship between genders gets swept up in the growing snowball of sin. It doesn't take long for this to morph into Lamech with his two wives (see Genesis 4:23). Not only is the sanctity of Lamech's marriage union corrupted by the introduction of a third person, but the writer offers a window into how patriarchy works in the mind of the patriarch. The names of Lamech's wives when translated from the Hebrew are "ornament"

(*Adah*) and "shadow" (*Zillah*). The image of God—the equal capacity of these women to exercise dominion—is suppressed. To Lamech, Adah exists to make him look better. In current-day lingo, she is eye candy or a trophy wife. Adah is window dressing. Zillah, on the other hand, is Lamech's trusty shadow. Always present, she serves to orient him and to remind him of his greatness. This is the natural outcome of pursuing human peace over God's shalom.

In Deuteronomy, as the people move from captivity into the land of promise, Moses hands down laws and statutes that prove the absolute shattering of shalom between men and women. The statutes are so specific that it is likely they were crafted to deal with common occurrences within the community. Notice the wreckage of the Fall:

> Suppose a man marries a woman, but after going in to her, he
> dislikes her and makes up charges against her, slandering her by
> saying, "I married this woman; but when I lay with her, I did not
> find evidence of her virginity." (22:13–14)

> But if the man meets the engaged woman in the open country,
> and the man seizes her and lies with her . . . (22:25)

> If a man meets a virgin who is not engaged, and seizes her and
> lies with her, and they are caught in the act . . . (22:28)

In a patriarchal society where women were bought and sold in marriage, where the highest praise a woman could hope for was that she was beautiful, where women could not own property, work an honest job, or divorce an abusive husband, people absorbed the shame of being seized, beaten, and raped. Today we understand rape for what it is, an act of domination. Rape is about power. It is not about lust, misguided love, or obsession. Rape is about power.

The opening of 2 Samuel 13 is revealing in this regard: "David's son Absalom had a beautiful sister whose name was Tamar; and David's son Amnon fell in love with her" (verse 1). In the next verse, the writer tells us Amnon fell ill because he found it impossible to do anything to his virgin sister, a royal, who was surrounded by other women and eunuch guards.

Love doesn't seek to do anything *to* the object of its affection. Love gives. Love protects. Love cultivates. Love serves. Amnon did not love Tamar. Rather, the author reveals the depth of the Fall's impact on the Hebrew culture of that day. The people were so far from Genesis 2's expectation of vulnerability, interdependence, mutual love, respect, and commitment that the storyteller, without further comment or disclaimer, frames Amnon's obsession as motivated by love.

Amnon set a trap for Tamar, feigning sickness and demanding that she feed him. He sent the servants away and seized her. In minutes, Tamar's sense of self—her dreams,

> Love doesn't seek to do anything *to* the object of its affection.

hopes, and potential to exercise dominion on earth—were crushed by one man's choice to force his way into her body, violating her sense of self, violating her capacity to exercise dominion over her own body, and violating the image of God within her.

In an instant, Tamar was reduced to the state of a childless widow, one of the worst forms of destitution within this patriarchal culture. Female virginity was the greatest prize, and without it no man would marry her.

With no husband, she could not secure shelter or food, and she could produce no male children to provide for her. According to Deuteronomy 22:28–29, Amnon should have been forced to marry Tamar, but he refused. His father, King David, chose to protect the perpetrator, his firstborn son, rather than the victim, his only daughter. Here the text reveals the deepseated cultural bias toward maleness and confirms the depth of male bias within the culture. A raped woman is punished; a rapist is protected.

Tamar's brother Absalom took her into his household. The text doesn't mention what became of Tamar, only that Absalom named his daughter after her and she was beautiful.

CURRENT-DAY WRECKAGE

America watched a security-camera video showing NFL player Ray Rice punch and knock out his fiancée, Janay Palmer, in a hotel elevator. We watched Rice get accepted into a pretrial intervention program. Then we watched the NFL vow to take domestic violence more seriously as it suspended Rice indefinitely. We watched Rice appeal the suspension and win. And we watched Rice return to the league as if nothing had happened, though no team has picked him. That didn't deter Janay, who married him months after she was assaulted.[3]

In 2013, the US Department of Justice issued a report on its National Crime Victimization Survey. Most of us never heard about it, but the numbers tell a story. That year, 1,116,090 Americans suffered domestic violence. More than 300,000 cases of rape and sexual assault were reported.[4] All told, more than one million people suffered the same domination and humiliation that Janay suffered. It repulsed and enraged us. And we accept it every day.

The United Nations defines gender-based violence as any act that results in "physical, sexual or psychological harm or suffering to women, including threats of such acts, coercion or arbitrary deprivations of liberty, whether occurring in public or in private life."[5] It is commonly understood that the violence results from power disparities based on gender roles and is usually interlinked with other forms of discrimination or oppression.

The Intersections of Violence

In a 2011 report to the UN General Assembly on gender-based violence, Rashida Manjoo pointed out that poverty is both "a cause and a consequence" of violence. Because most of the world's poor also are ethnic minorities within their states and communities, the condition of poverty is much harder to overcome. It is tied to identity—something unearned—as opposed to character or actions, which women can control. As a result, these women are far more likely to endure a lifetime of violence.[6]

In the United States, nowhere has the intersection of gender- and race-based oppression been more pronounced than in the indigenous and African American communities. Historically, indigenous women suffered rape at the hands of settlers, at the hands of soldiers during the Indian removals of the Southeast, and throughout the western Indian wars of the mid- to late nineteenth century. African American slaves suffered rape at the hands of their masters and enslaved men. Patriarchal southern culture treated all women, black and white, as property or chattel. Yet rape against enslaved black women was a part of the machine of the southern slavocracy.

In *Rape and Sexual Power in Early America,* Sharon Block offers an in-depth look at the culture of rape in early America. "For white women, patriarchy held out the possibility of providing protection from or remedy for sexual assaults. For nonwhite and other marginalized women, protective patriarchs were, at best, absent figures or, at worst, able to use their status to sexually oppress with impunity. . . . Placing these erased women back into the story of sexual coercion reveals that the exclusion of women of color from the status of rape victim was a crucial feature of American racialization of rape through not only legal prosecution, but also the privileges afforded to whiteness."[7]

THE UNMASKING OF GLOBAL GENDER-BASED VIOLENCE

In recent years, Americans witnessed the unmasking of several US military leaders who were charged with protecting the women in their ranks. The leaders were revealed to be perpetrators of sexual assault.[8] And around the world, the United Nations and nongovernmental organizations brought global forms of gender-based oppression to light through advocacy against female genital mutilation, child marriages, rape as a weapon of war, human trafficking, and the disparate impacts of climate change on women.

These things are not happening apart from the church. In fact, they often are happening inside churches. The Pew Research Center reported that in 2014, 70 percent of Americans identified as Christians.[9] The Centers for Disease Control and Prevention conducted a survey in 2010 that revealed that one in three women (and one-quarter of all men) in the United States have been victims of rape, physical violence, or stalking.[10] Yet when LifeWay Ministries conducted a national survey of pastors asking what percentage of their congregants they believe have been victims of sexual or gender-based violence, the largest majority (37 percent) estimated that less than half had experienced that pain.[11] Those numbers don't add up.

Where does the gap between perception and reality come from? Perhaps it's a symptom of the culture of patriarchy that thrives within church cultures and structures: male-dominated staff teams, male-dominated pastoral teams, and structural hierarchies that find few if any women in public leadership perpetuate male-dominated perspectives. If women aren't in the room to speak about a different experience of life, then that experience will likely be considered irrelevant.

But apart from male-dominated pastoral teams, let's say a woman is raped by her husband, a church usher. She asks the pastor to intervene. According to the LifeWay study, "Research indicates that abused women who seek help from untrained clergy typically find themselves in a worse situation than before." The survey explains, "A large majority (62 percent) of pastors surveyed say they have responded to sexual or domestic violence by providing couples or marriage counseling. This is considered a potentially dangerous or even potentially lethal response."[12]

Women and men who are victims of sexual and gender-based violence are sitting in church pews across the country. They suffer in silence. And when their pain surfaces, we are not prepared to deal with it.

Another insidious outcome of patriarchy is what it does to the way women and girls view themselves. Like Lamech's two wives, named Ornament (Adah) and Shadow (Zillah), women living under the press of patriarchy are surrounded with traditions, images, cultural norms, and social structures that reinforce the idea that women are not fully human. They do not bear God's image; only men do. They were not created to exercise dominion. They were created to be dominated by men.

We grow up and strive to take up as little space as possible. We mute our voices and fade into the background.

The only way a woman is allowed to take up space in patriarchal culture is if she adorns herself in ways that serve men's sexual appetites. The pornography and sex-trafficking industries attest to that. According to a 2014 national study by the Barna Group, 64 percent of men in the United States view pornography at least once a month. Christian men view pornography at the same rate, 64 percent, at least monthly.[13] Likewise, the International Labour Organization estimates that 4.5 million people are trapped in the global sex trade. The sex trade in the United States brings in profits to the tune of $39.9 million in Denver and $290 million in Atlanta, according to the Urban Institute.[14]

It is time for the church to stand up and say "No more" to the subjugation of half the world—half of the image of God in the world.

RESTORED BY TRUTH AND REPENTANCE

One of the first acts of the Holy Spirit at Pentecost was to include women in a public demonstration of the presence of God. A wind rushed down and tongues of fire rested on the heads of the Jesus followers huddled in an upper room. They were hiding from any who might identify them as people connected to the crucified Christ, but now they moved into the streets (see Acts 2:1–12).

Then Peter quoted the prophet Joel as he interpreted for the crowd what they were witnessing:

In the last days it will be, God declares,
 that I will pour out my Spirit upon all flesh,
  and your sons and daughters shall prophesy. . . .
Even upon my slaves, both men and women,

in those days I will pour out my Spirit;

and they shall prophesy. (verses 17–18)

God had broken into the order of this world ruled by empire, colonization, and patriarchy. God broke in by coming to both men and women. Men and women will exercise dominion, and in Acts 2, it was happening!

The Samaritan woman at the well was transformed in one interaction with Jesus and became the first evangelist in history (see John 4:1–42). Jesus showed mercy to the woman caught in adultery and told the men who brought her to the square to stone her: "Let anyone among you who is without sin be the first to throw a stone at her" (John 8:7). They laid down their stones and walked away. To the woman, he said, "Neither do I condemn you. Go your way, and from now on do not sin again" (verse 11). Jesus empowered the woman who had bled for twelve years. She lived in isolation outside the city walls, as custom commanded. When she pushed through the crowd to touch Jesus's garment, she was healed. But the woman's physical healing was not enough for him. He brought her to the center of the crowd and honored her by listening to her story. He called her "daughter" and empowered her socially by claiming her as his own family (see Luke 8:43–48).

Luke opened his gospel by highlighting a woman's interpretation of the theological significance of Jesus. Through Mary's *Magnificat,* Luke framed the proclamation of the coming Messiah as the beginning of a social and structural reversal. He also wrote the names of the women into the story of Jesus: "Then they remembered his words, and returning from the tomb, they told all this to the eleven and to all the rest. Now it was Mary Magdalene, Joanna, Mary the mother of James, and the other women with them who told this to the apostles." (24:8–10). And let us not forget that these women were women of color marginalized twice—once as Jews within the Roman imperial structure and a second time by their own men.

Paul often is quoted within streams of the Christian church that believe patriarchy is God's good intention. Traditionalists are known to quote Paul's first letter to the church in Corinth: "But any woman who prays or prophesies with her head unveiled disgraces her head—it is one and the same thing as having her head shaved. For if a woman will not veil herself, then she should cut off her hair; but if it is disgraceful for a woman to have her hair cut off or to be shaved, she should wear a veil" (11:5–6). They may also quote Paul's first letter to his apprentice, Timothy: "Let a woman learn in silence with full submission. I permit no woman to teach or to have authority over a man; she is to keep silent" (2:11–12).

> To take these words as doctrine is to ignore the full counsel of Paul's teachings and the ways he interacted with and promoted women leaders.

The problem with lifting these quotes out of context and making them serve as a doctrinal tenant of the church is that Paul did not write them as doctrine. He wrote the statements as context-specific advice to help two churches deal with issues arising within their communities. He drew on his own leadership traditions, shaped by culture and personal preference. And he applied the traditions to a particular time in a particular place. To take these words as doctrine is to ignore the full counsel of Paul's teachings and the ways he interacted with and promoted women leaders.

In her book *Malestrom: Manhood Swept into the Currents of a Changing World,* Carolyn Custis James marvels at Paul's conversion and its impact on how he engaged with women. She points out that Paul's conversion catapulted him not only across ethnic barriers into ministry with gentiles but also across gender barriers into equal partnership with women.

Custis James wrote, "The apostle Paul is the unexpected Exhibit A of the fact that men and boys who follow Jesus are radical like the Jesus they follow. They defy the maelstrom and embrace the freeing life-giving power of the gospel. They are not confined by patriarchy or any other cultural definition of what it means to be a man, but instead reclaim their Edenic call to image God."[15]

Paul often announced at the beginning of his letters that he was an apostle, a necessary proclamation for one whose apostleship started after the days of Jesus. As such, one of the most fascinating greetings he sends can be found in his letter to the church in Rome: "Greet Andronicus and Junia, my relatives who were in prison with me; they are prominent among the apostles, and they were in Christ before I was" (Romans 16:7). The role of apostles was to lead the church in particular cities or regions. Paul demonstrates great respect for Junia's leadership and highlights the fact that she suffered with him in prison.[16]

Paul partnered with many women he considered colaborers: Lydia was the leader of the first church plant in Europe (see Acts 16:40), and he wrote of Euodia and Syntyche, colaborers in Philippi (see Philippians 4:2). Ministering in Rome there was Phoebe the deacon (see Romans 16:1), Priscilla the lead evangelist (see Romans 16:3; Acts 18:18, 26; 2 Timothy 4:19), and Persis, Paul's dear friend and colaborer (see Romans 16:12).

In Galatians, Paul leveraged his cultural power as a male to destroy male dominance within the church. His statement on baptism became the baptismal liturgy for the early church: "As many of you as were baptized into Christ have clothed yourselves with Christ. There is no longer Jew or Greek, there is no longer slave or free, there is no longer male or female; for all of you are one in Christ Jesus" (3:27–28).

At the heart of the very good news of the gospel is the reversal of the Fall. With that reversal, Jesus's death and resurrection paved the way for patriarchy to be crushed. This made way for the full acknowledgment of the image of God in women and men.

RESTORING EZER

All the way back to the days of slavery in America, every woman in my mother's direct line of ancestry suffered sexual violence. This includes me. My great-aunt died in the woods after being raped by her uncle. My third great-grandmother, the last adult slave in our family, bore seventeen children by five "husbands." Family lore says that her husbands kept dying or being sold away. It also is possible that she was forced to breed children on a plantation in South Carolina. She herself was half-white, likely the product of a rape. Most of the women in our family suffered in silence, and some suffered again when they raised their voices to name their perpetrators. Fathers, cousins, even sisters and pastors minimized the pain and chastised the crushed ones for disturbing the peace.

The image of God was broken in me at a young age at the hands of a family member. It was crushed again at the hands of men in the evangelical church who told me I was created to follow, not to lead. They told me that as a woman, I should not be able to co-lead a prayer group with a man. Another told me I could not lead worship if a man was there to lead. I internalized the devil's lie that dominion was divinely reserved for men.

Healing came gradually. I met the biblical character Priscilla and was blown away that she was the leader in her partnership with her husband. Paul affirmed that by listing her first in his final greetings in 2 Timothy 4:19. She became my hero. Then I listened to a sermon by megachurch pastor Bill Hybels, who shared that he was concerned that his daughter, a gifted preacher, would not be able to flourish to her fullest capacity within the patriarchal culture of the church.

What will it take to restore *ezer* ("aid; help") in the church and in the world? How do followers of Jesus restore the image of God in the world through holy disruption of cultural, social, systemic, and structural norms? Here are a few practices I have witnessed that aim to restore the very goodness in interpersonal, systemic, and structural relationships between women and men.

Listen to the stories of women. A few months ago, I sat in a room with evangelical men and women leaders of color. Aware of the male-dominant cultures of both evangelicalism and communities of color, the leaders in the group set aside time for the women to share stories of subjugation and healing within the evangelical church. Each of us took three minutes to share our story. After each woman had spoken, the men asked clarifying questions. Men's mouths dropped as they realized they had witnessed subjugation and not been aware of it. They had systemically or structurally participated in the dismissal of the image of God in their sisters. And they had been party to injustice, even while working for justice.

Lament. There is real pain just beneath the surface. Women are suffering, often in silence, at the hands of physical or mental abusers and sexual abusers or under reign of cultural patriarchy. The discussion of gender-based violence is a fairly new one for most of the church. Before we allow ourselves to retreat behind protective dogma, we must allow ourselves to feel the pain of our sisters and brothers. And we must allow ourselves to grasp the impact that male domination has had on the witness of the church in the world. We must face it, own it, and grieve it. I recommend Soong-Chan Rah's book *Prophetic Lament: A Call for Justice in Troubled Times* as a good next step to understanding the healing power of lament.

Confess. It is not enough just to see the problem. We must also own our part in it, both men and women. We must examine and interrogate our theological beliefs about gender roles. We must also examine and interrogate our language and the systems and structures we build and maintain. Does our language reflect the male and female nature of the image of God? Does it cultivate, protect, and serve the co-dominion of males and females? Are the systems and structures we build and maintain actively and consciously cultivating, protecting, and serving the image of God in women?

Repent. Go and sin no more. We must mindfully move through the world conscious of the ways that patriarchy is a fallen construct in the kingdom of men. It is at war with the Kingdom of God. We must forsake it and choose God and God's way to peace.

Reflection Exercise

If you are a woman who has suffered the suppression of the image of God in your marriage, your church, your family, and/or your community, then here is a reflection exercise for you:

1. Close your eyes and ask God to show you the part of yourself that feels strong, the part of your voice that feels rich, full, and like it might have something stored up that is worthy of taking up space in the world.

2. Sit in that space. Take note of how it feels in this strong space. This full, weighty space.

3. Ask God to show you how God sees your strength. Listen as God whispers to your soul, "This is very good."

4. Pray. Thank God for making you a woman who is strong, full, worthy of taking up space, and created with the call and capacity to exercise dominion.

Finally, I offer you advice that an older, wiser woman offered me. She said, "Lisa, you will flourish when you stop apologizing for your power and live fully into the woman God created you to be." She was right.

Shalom and Creation

I clicked through the pages of the *New York Times* website, just scanning headlines, when I came across a picture I couldn't comprehend. I looked more closely and saw black people in torn and dirty clothes. They were walking in a desolate place, searching for something. The caption read, "In a garbage dump in Port-au-Prince, people recently scavenged for food." The year was 2008, two years before the devastating Haiti earthquake.[1]

Why were people searching for food in a garbage dump? Because soil erosion, resulting from extreme deforestation and mass monocropping during the colonial era, as well as current impacts of climate change, have made farming extremely difficult in Haiti.[2] Also, per the *New York Times* article, subsidized foods from wealthy nations are sold to developing nations such as Haiti at a price that knocks local farmers out of competition. This makes Haitians even more dependent on food imports. About half of Haiti's food is imported, including 80 percent of the nation's staple, rice.[3] In 2008, the global food market experienced a major price hike in food imports coming from wealthy nations. The hike sparked food riots in developing nations around the globe, including Haiti.

To get by, the poorest of the poor have taken to eating mud. Patties made of mud, oil, and sugar calm the stomachs of hungry humans.[4]

How did we get to a place where our neighbors have to eat dirt to survive? And where does God want us to go?

THE BETRAYAL

I grew up with five brothers and sisters. My older brother and I often were put in charge of our other siblings when my mother and dad were out of the house. It was our job to make sure everyone did their chores. In the same way, God puts humans—the youngest sibling of creation—in charge of our older sibling creatures. It is our responsibility to keep these relationships intact.

Earlier we learned that God has told us what very goodness looks like (see Genesis 1:26–31). What God calls very good is the wellness of all the relationships God created in the beginning. This includes the relationship between humanity and the rest of creation. The sun, the moon, and stars serve humanity and the rest of creation by providing sustenance for our bodies and light for night travel. The stars tell people—especially in ancient agrarian cultures—when to wake, sleep, harvest, and sow. Plants serve animals by offering themselves for food (see Genesis 1:30). We see humanity serving and protecting the ground when God calls humanity to till (*abad* = to serve) and keep (*shamar* = to protect) the earth (see Genesis 2:15) and to serve the animals by naming them (see Genesis 2:19–20).

As those called to exercise dominion, humanity will be held accountable for what happens to God's masterpiece, the earth.

And as we serve, protect, and cultivate our siblings in creation, very goodness looks like justice and peace, truth and mercy, honor and humility among humans. We are made in God's likeness, but we are not God. We are well aware that there are only two kinds of beings, creature and Creator. We are creature. God is God; we are not. Therefore, we are not free to do as we please with creation. Our dominion must bow to the will of God. And if it is to be in the image of God's dominion, then it must be grounded in love. Love binds all creation together.

God issued one command in the Garden of Eden, and it was connected to the land: "You may freely eat of every tree of the garden; but of the tree of the knowledge of good and evil you shall not eat, for in the day that you eat of it you shall die" (Genesis 2:16–17). As we discussed in chapter 3, there was only one boundary given to hu-

> Love binds all creation together.

manity in Eden. The Tree of the Knowledge of Good and Evil gave humans the chance to demonstrate their love for God by trusting God's words and intent and choosing God's way to peace. God issued the warning, and it was (and is) an experience of evil to distrust God.

God told humanity, "Don't do it! I want you and your children and your children's children to know shalom. I want you to know a lush and lavish world, a world where all relationships are very good, a world without people climbing on garbage heaps to find food, a world without droughts and water wars and deforestation and enmity between you and your older sibling creatures. You see this world I've created? When you consider it, you see who I am. I am lavish with you. I am extravagant in my love for you. You need not fear me. I will never exploit you."

Then the serpent sidled up to the woman and man and drilled the first crack in humanity's relationship with God. The humans trusted themselves and their own way to peace. They trusted the words of the serpent, which said the way to peace is to put God's way aside and grab peace for themselves. The best that human peace can offer is broken peace. In Genesis 3, every relationship God had declared very good was shattered, including humanity's relationship with the rest of creation.

The LORD God said to the serpent,

"Because you have done this,
    cursed are you among all animals
    and among all wild creatures;
upon your belly you shall go,
    and dust you shall eat
    all the days of your life.
I will put enmity between you and the woman,
    and between your offspring and hers;
he will strike your head,
    and you will strike his heel." (verses 14–15)

We often hear this verse interpreted as a foreshadowing of Jesus's victory over Satan through the Resurrection, and that may be true. But in a very tangible sense, this is the first time in Scripture that we see an animal striking a human being.

A few verses later, the ground is cursed:

And to the man he said,

"Because you have listened to the voice of your wife,
    and have eaten of the tree

about which I commanded you,

'You shall not eat of it,'

cursed is the ground because of you;

in toil you shall eat of it all the days of your life;

thorns and thistles it shall bring forth for you;

and you shall eat the plants of the field." (verses 17–18)

It wasn't supposed to be this way. The earth is cursed because of humanity's lack of trust in God. Because we chose our own peace above the peace of all, creation suffers. Thus, our relationship with the land functions as a kind of sin meter in a post-Fall world. When we see cracked earth and swollen bellies, we can know someone has sinned in this place.

People crawling over garbage dumps in search of food is an indicator of an active break in relationship between humanity and the rest of creation. Year after year in Haiti, planters planted the same crop in the same soil. It depleted the soil of nutrients and decreased crop yield. Colonists cut down the vast forests to make room for crops. After Haitians revolted and gained independence, France collected restitution in the form of timber. Later, speculators and planters pushed poor people to the forested mountainsides. Over the years, Haitians cut down more trees for gardens and for fuel; less than 4 percent of Haiti's forests remains. The loss of forests has led to severe soil erosion.[5]

The humans chose not to trust God and God's words and afterward tried to hide from God. In response to their shame, God killed an animal: "And the LORD God made garments of skins for the man and for his wife, and clothed them" (verse 21). The creature dangled in God's hands as God ripped it in two, spilling blood for the first time on earth. God killed his own creation to cover humanity's shame. Death entered the world. Humanity was driven from the garden as a cherubim guarded the way to the Tree of Life. The guard kept the humans from eating of the tree and living forever in these deteriorating conditions. Sin had separated us from God, from the rest of creation, and from life itself. The sin-stained mantra of human peace is "Our peace at the expense of their peace!" And what does it get us?

THE IMPACT TODAY

The relationship between humanity and the rest of creation was broken, and we see the results all around us. The environment suffers because we chose not to trust God and to seek our own peace instead.

Climate Change

California is experiencing the worst drought in twelve hundred years.[6] Standing in a brown field that should have been buried under several feet of snow on the first day of Earth Month, California governor Jerry Brown said, "It's a different world. We have to act differently."[7]

California is an object lesson on the impacts of climate change for the world. It is one of the most diverse swaths of land in the world, boasting mountains, beaches, deserts, and forests. Explosive population growth has led to rural, urban, and suburban sprawl. Among its residents we see the super-rich and the super-poor. Among the poorest, California's farm workers have borne the brunt of the fallout from the state's struggle with climate change. Farmers have had to lay off seventeen thousand workers due to climate-related losses.[8]

In a survey, the National Medical Association found that doctors are citing climate-related conditions among the factors affecting the health of patients. Included are injuries due to severe weather events, chronic diseases intensified by increased air pollution, more widespread allergy symptoms, heat-related conditions, increased incidents of infections such as Lyme disease and West Nile virus, diarrhea caused by food or water, and mental-health issues. The doctors also identified groups most likely to be affected by climate change, including people with chronic diseases, people living near or below the poverty line, children from birth to age four, adults older than sixty, and people of color.[9]

Globally, women bear most of the burden because they represent the majority of the world's poor. Short-term effects of climate change, such as landslides, floods, and hurricanes, as well as long-term effects, such as gradual environmental degradation, exert a profound impact on the lives and livelihoods of women.[10] Increasingly common and increasingly intense climate events disrupt the ability of poor people to survive.

Imagine living in a land where there is no water. That's what it was like in Syria from 2006 to 2009. The nation suffered the worst drought in modern times, triggered by a century-long increase in heat and dryness in the region. The conditions were caused by climate change resulting from human activities, scientists say. A *New York Times* report explained how the dominoes fell: "[Scientists] cited studies that showed that the extreme dryness, combined with other factors, including misguided agricultural and water-use policies of the Syrian government, caused crop failures that led to the migration of as many as 1.5 million people from rural to urban areas. This in turn added to social stresses that eventually resulted in the uprising against President Bashar al-Assad in March 2011."[11]

Imagine watching your nation dry up in just five years. And imagine watching your nation's leaders making choices about land and water use that only make things worse. Now imagine getting to the point where there is no food in the stores and no water flowing from kitchen faucets. This is what happened to the people of Syria. They tried to topple al-Assad and found themselves in a multiyear war that displaced more than four million people, tossing them into extreme poverty and triggering the greatest migration through Europe since World War II. And here's a connection we rarely make: all these shifts cleared the way for the rise of ISIS in the region.

Other Betrayals

The genocide in Darfur started as a fight between herdsmen and farmers over access to water during the drought of the 1980s. Muammar Gaddafi of Libya fanned the flames of ethnic hatred, framing the fight as an ethnic Arab–black battle. It was not. It was about water. Soon people were killing each other en masse. Then the land became unusable. It was dry and barren because the people who were stewarding the land had been displaced or slaughtered.[12]

I drove through Croatia on the Balkan Pilgrimage for Reconciliation in 2004. We were stunned by the beauty of sunflower fields that extended for miles. We were so moved by the beauty that our group broke into song, worshiping God, on our way to talk with Croatian farmers who had endured the Croatian War of 1991–1995. We arrived in Osijek, piled out of the bus, and crowded into a conference room. We shared with the director of a community-development organization that we were overwhelmed by the beauty of the sunflowers. She explained, "Yes. The sunflowers are so tall and plentiful because no one can go into the fields to plow them. The fields are full of mines."

In Warren County, North Carolina, the residents of a small, predominantly black town learned that a hazardous-waste landfill was slated for their community. According to a report posted on the US Department of Energy website, the state of North Carolina had considered several possible sites before choosing this African American community. Neighbors organized and pastors and congressional representatives joined the fight to keep the landfill out. But they lost the battle. The landfill was opened, and the environmental justice movement was born. Within years, several studies were commissioned, most notably the United Church of Christ 1987 study "Toxic Waste and Race." The study found that race was the most significant factor in determining where toxic-waste facilities were located. Three out of five African Americans live in a community with a hazardous-waste facility.[13] The health impacts of these toxins include increased incidents of cancer, liver failure, and slowed growth or development.[14]

When we deprive people of the ability to exercise dominion (agency) and then we exploit the land, the image of God is crushed on earth. God does not reign in that place, and the damage to creation stands as a witness to our rebellion. We were meant to exercise dominion over the rest of creation, not over each other. We were meant to be protectors, cultivators, and servants of the land, not its exploiters. We were meant to maintain the boundaries of God's systems, which benefit all, not to create systems that benefit a few at the expense of the rest.

> We were meant to be protectors, cultivators, and servants of the land, not its exploiters.

Paul tells us in Romans 8:19–22, "For the creation waits with eager longing for the revealing of the children of God; for the creation was subjected to futility, not of its own will but by the will of the one who subjected it, in hope that the creation itself will be set free from its bondage to decay and will obtain the freedom of the glory of the children of God. We know that the whole creation has been groaning in labor pains until now."

Creation has been subject to futility. Fruitfulness, purpose, and abundant life are blocked by the curse, blocked by human sin, blocked by the younger siblings that God called to serve, protect, and cultivate the elder creatures. Locked in a cycle of fruitless struggle, creation groans as it longs for the children of God to be revealed. They are the ones who trust God, who choose God's way. And when that day comes, creation will be redeemed.

This is the state of creation at the end of Genesis 3, but it is not the end of the story. God says if we humble ourselves and repent, God will heal the land.

HEALING THE LAND

The people of ancient Israel cried out, "Restore us again, O God of our salvation, and put away your indignation toward us. . . . Let me hear what God the LORD will speak, for he will speak peace [shalom] to his people, to his faithful, to those who turn to him in their hearts" (Psalm 85:4, 8). God told the people that God would restore shalom. God painted a picture of all the ingredients of shalom springing from creation. Love and truth will meet; justice and peace will kiss. God will restore what is good (*tov*): the wellness of all relationships in creation (shalom).

Jesus stood in a synagogue and read from a scroll a proclamation of the year of jubilee. It is a proclamation that the poor, the marginalized, and the oppressed will be restored to full dignity. Text from the prophet Isaiah contains an allusion to the two trees in the Garden of Eden and to God's promise made in Psalm 85: "For as the earth brings forth its shoots, and as a garden causes what is sown in it to spring up, so the LORD God will cause righteousness and praise to spring up before all the nations" (Isaiah 61:11). The Kingdom of God will bring the restoration of all creation.

After Jesus read from the scroll, he sat down and said to the people, "Today this scripture has been fulfilled in your hearing" (Luke 4:21). In other words, "Right here, right now, it's on!"

In the person of Jesus, the Kingdom of God had broken into the world. This means the reversal of the Fall is imminent. Creation will be restored.

In the course of Jesus's life on earth, he confronted the desolation of the Fall in the moments before he preached his first sermon. He spent forty days in the wilderness, the place of desolation, the place where the thorns and thistles of Genesis 3 made their home. He confronted the desolation and overcame it. And Jesus walked on water, much like the Holy Spirit hovered over the water in Genesis 1. Jesus slept in a boat, absolutely at peace, demonstrating no fear of the deep. When the winds whipped the waters, he commanded the wind, "*Ereine*! Be still!" *Ereine* is the Greek version of the Hebrew word *shalom*. Be still (*siopao*) means forced, involuntary stillness.

Like Elohim over the deep, the One who created the sea monsters, Jesus revealed that he is the source of our peace (*shalom, ereine*). We can be at peace when Jesus is near. Jesus exercised dominion over creation to serve humanity. He multiplied bread and fish to feed thousands, and he smeared mud on the eyes of a blind man to give him sight (see John 9:1–12).

Later Jesus was crucified on a tree. God—the Creator of the tree—was nailed to it. The original sin of humanity was committed in relation to a tree, the Tree of the Knowledge of Good and Evil. Now the redemption of humanity and the reversal of the Fall happens in relation to a tree. Then Jesus conquered death, opening his own grave. And in the end there is only one tree, the Tree of Life. The tree's leaves are for the healing of the nations (see Revelation 22:1–2).

Reconciling with Creation in the Here and Now

What does reconciliation with creation look like in our lives? Each of us has the ability to ask God to give us the answer.

Humility

"If my people who are called by my name humble themselves, pray, seek my face, and turn from their wicked ways, then I will hear from heaven, and will forgive their sin and heal their land" (2 Chronicles 7:14). At the root of it, we're dealing with a spiritual condition. And lack of humility manifests itself in the way we interact with others. The first requirement of reconciliation with the land is humility. We must be willing to identify our pride and admit the truth about ourselves.

We buy into Western pride when we separate ourselves from the rest of creation, in essence claiming to be non-creatures. If we are non-creatures, then we are gods. If we are gods, it's not hard to believe that we cannot sin against creation. We can only make choices that inherently improve creation's conditions. We must confess this sin-filled belief and repent. We must place ourselves back in the family of creatures. And we must agree with God that the fact that we are creature is very good.

Humility leads us to acknowledge that God has placed wisdom in the minds and hearts of cultures across the globe—and we need it all to survive. If the world must rely on Western culture to fix the earth, then we are doomed. The Western march toward so-called civilization is what introduced colonization, monocropping, deforestation, and inequitable protection of people even as it exploited the land. The developed world must humble itself and turn toward the ones Jesus would call "the least of these"—women, indigenous people, and small family farmers. From these people we can glean the wisdom God has given them through the land.

Advocate for Just Systems and Structures Through Just Policy

Humanity's most basic vocation is to exercise dominion over (to serve, protect, and cultivate the wellness of) the rest of creation. Reconciliation will require deep examination of our personal and communal habits, our city systems and structures, and our national energy policies. For the past two decades, the world has waited for the United States to take measures to decrease its greenhouse gas emissions. Each time the international community has come together since 2000, the United States has failed to take a leading role to curb global practices that cause climate change.[15] In December 2015, the United States stood with 195 other nations and committed to do its part to curb climate change. We must support the Paris Agreement and press our federal, state, and local legislators to find innovative ways to abide by it.

Another great indicator of the presence of unjust environmental policies is the presence of racial and economic inequity with regard to land use, air and water quality, and food distribution. We must ask the question of each habit, practice, and policy, "Is this action or policy serving me/us at the expense of the wellness of our siblings in creation?" If it is, then we must repent and find another way.

Individual Practices

First, practice generosity (see Mark 6:30-44). One of the great temptations of our time is to live in fear that our resources will run out. Climate change exacerbates that fear. But the story of Jesus feeding five thousand people from five loaves of bread and two fish offers a powerful reminder. There is enough. God is the Creator of all of it. God can feed five thousand people from one child's lunch. But what if it wasn't a hocus-pocus kind of miracle? What if God fed five thousand people by leading those who had brought a lunch to share what they had? What if the people passed the basket and put in what they had and at the end they had bread and fish left over? That, too, would be a miracle—the miracle of generosity.

Second, practice simple living by forsaking overconsumption in favor of making sure all have enough (see Exodus 16:4). One of the greatest lies of our culture is "I buy, therefore I am." Politicians call citizens "consumers." We are not consumers. Consumption is not a part of our identity and worth. This lie drives us to consume more than any other nation on earth. As a result, we send more carbon into the atmosphere than anyone else. We must fight the lie that our worth comes from our ability to consume. When we're tempted to consume more than we need, it's time to think about manna. God provided manna for the freed slaves who were wandering in the wilderness. It fell from heaven. God told the people to take what they needed and leave the rest. If they took more manna than they needed, it would rot in their possession. Let's learn from the lesson of manna.

Third, practice dependence on God for basic needs (see Matthew 6:9-11). The Lord's Prayer contains this profound line: "Give us this day our daily bread." During my summer in the Balkans, I found that people shopped for enough to cover one day's meals. They had small neighborhood stores or farmers' markets, and they did not have a tradition of storing up food. Rather, they planned each meal, savoring time together at mealtime. What would it be like if we focused on one meal at a time, savoring it, sharing it with family and friends, and thanking God for the time and food being shared? I have a feeling we (and the rest of creation) would find more peace.

Fourth, practice reciprocity (see Luke 6:38; 2 Corinthians 9:6–11; Galatians 6:7–9). Reciprocity is the process of receiving and restoring. In his book *Shalom and the Community of Creation,* Randy Woodley says, "One of the most basic examples of this kind of reciprocity is how the exchange of oxygen and carbon dioxide between plants and animals keeps us all living."[16] Woodley describes the Native American Harmony Way, a practice of respect for all creation and the web of relationships that connects us. Reciprocity is the intentional act of restoring what is taken. In Scripture, the result is shalom. A simple example comes from a common native practice of always giving back to land that has been harvested. While a common practice among farmers, the practice of reciprocity is only beginning to take hold on larger scales. Households, cities, states, and nations are beginning to take stock of the carbon imprints left by their consumption of food and energy. They are intentionally offsetting carbon production by planting more trees and gardens, integrating local farming into urban food systems, and encouraging the use of nondisposable items for shopping and leisure.[17] What would it look like if every household, town, and city made reciprocity a value as it ordered life together? We would always seek balanced relationship with the land, giving and taking, planting and harvesting. Over time we would experience scripture's promise: abundance.

Reflection Exercise

Consider the four practices listed above: generosity, forsaking overconsumption, dependence on God, and reciprocity.

Have you ever experienced any of these practices in your life? How did it feel?

Which one practice could you imagine integrating into your life today? What is the greatest challenge you might face as you implement it?

Is there a friend or group that might be interested in committing to grow in this practice with you? Ask them today, and begin restoring very good relationships with the rest of creation right where you are.

Finally, imagine yourself sitting on the side of a mountain. You are so overcome with the beauty of creation that you begin to hum your favorite song. You sing with eyes closed as your hands begin to rise up to the heavens. You find yourself worshiping God. Suddenly, you see that tree branches also are reaching to the sky and swaying in the wind. Ravens are playing nearby, swirling, dipping, and gliding on your simple melody.

Do you see it? You are not the only one worshiping God. You have simply joined creation's worship of its Creator.

Shalom for Broken Families

Let me introduce you to a couple we'll call Robert and Lydia. In their blended family, they have two children: a girl and a boy. To the outside world they look like the perfect family, and if you knew them you would agree they are impressive people. Robert produces a local television news program; Lydia is an artist. Her work is featured in shop windows and art galleries around town.

Within a few years of their marriage, anyone who looked closely could see cracks beginning to form in the couple's facade.

From the outside, observers could see that Lydia's daughter had grown distant and stopped engaging with the rest of the family. Robert's son had been the life of any party, but then he disappeared from the home. And Lydia, once full of creative ideas for fun learning experiences for her daughter, also had withdrawn. She was silent when she was home, but she was rarely at home.

Behind closed doors, shalom had been plundered. Robert and Lydia discovered that Robert's son had raped Lydia's daughter. Although the son was immediately put out of the house, it was decided that no charges would be pressed. The family stayed together, the violated daughter coped the best she could, and they never discussed it again. But not talking about it didn't mean the problem had gone away. The accumulated pain crashed down decades later when it became known that the pattern of abuse was repeating in the next generation.

It wasn't supposed to be this way.

In Genesis 1, God created man and woman in the image of God, with equal call and capacity to exercise dominion. In Genesis 2, two individuals became one flesh, and God created the family. This serves as the most powerful example of creation's web of connectedness.

After the Fall, we see the immediate distortion of the family unit. The natural repercussion of coming out from under the covering of God's shalom is broken trust between the man and woman (see Genesis 3:12) and pain in childbearing for women (see verse 16). The woman's desire is for her husband (see verse 16), but the man is focused on the work of tilling dry earth (see verses 17–19). We see the ways in which the break in their love relationship with God damaged the rest of creation (see verses 15, 17–18). Finally, death entered the world, creating a natural end to the life of the family unit and the creation of generations (see verse 24). It wasn't long before the sin of the parents was reflected in the next generations.

When Abel brought the fatty portions of the firstlings of his flock as an offering to God and Cain brought an offering of the fruit of the ground to God, Abel's offering to God was accepted with high regard. But the text says God gave no regard to the offering brought by Cain, Abel's brother.

Was God a stickler for following regulations? I don't think so. Abel's offering required trust in God, trust that even if he gave God the very best that he had to offer, God would sustain him well on what he had left. Cain reserved the best for himself and gave God the leftovers. God didn't smite Cain for doing this; God simply made it known that God wasn't impressed. But here's the thing: Cain mistakenly interpreted God's lack of regard for his offering as a lack of regard for him as a person. God came to Cain to clarify things: "If you do well, will you not be accepted? And if you do not do well, sin is lurking at the door; its desire is for you, but you must master it" (Genesis 4:7).

In essence, God was saying, "You can follow in the footsteps of your parents, who rejected me and chose their own way to peace. You can store up the best portions from your labor and let your lack of trust in me lead you to play God with your life in your own way. Or you can do well by trusting me. You can demonstrate your love and trust by offering your first fruits. My love for you is constant, Cain, but I will not disregard what your actions communicate about your level of trust and love for me."

In the next breath, Cain said to Abel, "Let us go out to the field." The two did, and Cain killed his brother.

Sin is separation from God. Sin mastered Cain and drove him to the ultimate form of separation within creation—permanent separation from his brother. Murder is the execution of the image of God on earth. And as we have seen already, sin separates.

"Then the LORD said to Cain, 'Where is your brother Abel?' [Cain] said, 'I do not know; *am I my brother's keeper?*'" (verse 9). Remember, the Hebrew word for keeper is *shamar,* meaning "to protect." It is the same word the writer of Genesis 2 used to describe the vocation of humanity: "The LORD God took the man and put him in the garden of Eden to till and keep [protect] it" (verse 15). *Shamar* clarifies the picture of what it looks like to exercise dominion. It is not the kind of dominion that rules over but rather the kind that stewards, cultivates, and protects.

After Cain committed the first murder on earth, the ground opened up to receive Abel's blood. What a moment! The land itself stood in solidarity against injustice and served as a witness before God against Cain's oppression of Abel. Cain did not care for his brother, but the land cared. And like his parents before him, Cain's relationship with the ground was cursed.

Five generations later, Lamech boasted of killing a man who had wounded him (see Genesis 4:23). This was hardly a proportional response. Within seven generations of the garden, Lamech was the picture of oppression as he suppressed the image of God in others. The sin of domination snowballed through the generations. The overflowing goodness of the family was among the first casualties of the Fall.

When I interviewed Dr. Claudia Owens Shields, department chair of clinical psychology at the Chicago School of Professional Psychology, she explained, "General family systems theory says that anytime any one individual in the family is affected by something, it sends a ripple through the whole family."[1]

This understanding of the family is seen at the heart of the biblical concept of shalom. Injustice to any part of creation affects the whole. Likewise, there is no peace for the whole unless there is peace for each part. So the wellness of each family member benefits the whole. The same is true across generations.

> This understanding of the family is seen at the heart of the biblical concept of shalom.

Generations in a single family are connected across time. Speaking of idols, God commanded, "You shall not bow down to them or worship them; for I the LORD your God am a jealous God, punishing children for the iniquity of parents, to the third and the fourth generation of those who reject me, but showing steadfast love to the thousandth generation of those who love me and keep my commandments" (Exodus 20:5–6).

The Hebrew word for punish here is *paqad*, which means "to visit," "to bestow," or "to do judgment." It can be read as it is in the New Revised Standard Version as God punishing the children. But it also can mean that God allows the natural consequences of the parents' sin to affect families to the third and fourth generation. The second interpretation expresses what we understand of the nature of the Fall. Breaks in all the relationships in creation are not God's desired outcome; they are instead the natural outcomes of humanity's choosing its own way to peace. Claudia Owens Shields explained that families work in the same way. "In practical terms, a family is like a bicycle," she said. "If you take the chain off that bike, you can pedal all you want, but that bike isn't going anywhere . . . because that bicycle functions as a system. A family functions in the same way."[2]

FAMILY STRUCTURE IN THE BIBLE

In *An Introduction to the Hebrew Bible: A Thematic Approach,* the authors lay to rest any notion that Hebrew families resembled the Western concept of the family unit having a father, a mother, and two children. What's more, they say, the Hebrews didn't have any one standardized family structure. It evolved over time and adapted to meet economic, geographical, and social needs. The typical Hebrew household likely averaged between twelve and fifteen people, including the senior man and senior woman, their sons, their sons' spouses, and the grandchildren. The household also might include a relative whose previous household had been dissolved through death or trauma. Richer households might also include servants, slaves, concubines, military captives, and resident immigrants.

The Fall's deep impact is manifest in the patriarchal Hebrew family structure. Everyone and everything revolved around and was dependent on the senior male and his sons. In this structure, women have no value apart from their ability to add value to the man's household. The notion of equal dominion, seen in Genesis 1 and 2, is unthinkable in this structure. Nowhere is this clearer than in Hebrew families' understanding of sex within marriage. There was no category for rape because women and their bodies were considered the property of the men. In fact, paired husband-wife teams don't make up the foundation of the ancient Hebrew family. Instead, one dominant man takes a number of different women into his household and owns them. One or more of the women may come from among his kin or an allied household, but they were joined by slaves, servants, concubines, and other household dependents. All of these women often related to the senior male sexually and socially.[3]

MERRY DYSFUNCTION TO US

A few years ago, my mother came to visit during the Christmas holidays. She was newly separated from my stepfather. As a result, our family ritual of going to Mom and Dad's for Christmas was disrupted. For most women of my generation, that wouldn't be such a big deal. They would opt for staying home with their own families or they would take their families to the in-laws'. But I am not married. And while my year is full of travel, speaking, writing, and training others, when the holidays come, I'm reminded of the life I have not been able to live.

I can usually quiet the dream of having a husband and children with the fun of playing with nieces and nephews or the joy of cooking my favorite dish for the family. But this year it was just me and Mom, and neither of us felt like cooking. We went to several movies over the course of her weeklong visit. But I felt the emptiness and the loneliness of the changes brought by our broken family.

All things being equal, I could have focused on my mom's two failed marriages and blamed her for failing to demonstrate what healthy love looks like. I might have blamed both my father and my stepfather for choosing infidelity over family. And I suppose part of me does still linger there. But this isn't fiction, and all things are not equal for me. I am a black woman in the United States of America. That means my mother and father and their mothers and fathers and my brother and uncles and aunties and ancestors back to the other side of the Atlantic all navigated family systems that were severely hindered by outside forces: slavery, Jim Crow, housing discrimination, education discrimination, employment discrimination, and much more. The impacts of inside *and* outside forces play a significant role in shaping family structure.

According to a 2014 study by the Pew Research Center, marriage rates are falling for everyone, but no group is affected more than black Americans. "Among black adults ages 25 and older, the share who has never been married has quadrupled over the past half century—from 9% in 1960 to 36% in 2012."[4] For the sake of comparison, the study reports that the share of whites who have never married has doubled. The percentage of never-married whites went from virtually equal to blacks in 1960 (8 percent) to only half the rate of never-married blacks in 2012 (16 percent). In most groups, according to the study, men are more likely than women to have never been married. The major exception is within the black community.

"In 2012, roughly equal shares of black men (36%) and black women (35%) ages 25 and older had never been married."[5]

Reasons for the drop-off in marriage rates since the 1960s include higher education levels among women resulting in a greater capacity to support themselves and less financial dependence on a husband. Likewise, women who have never been married tend to have higher employment expectations of a potential spouse. But in the unstable job market of the past decade, men have found fewer opportunities for meaningful employment. Add to this that women who have never married tend to have higher education levels than men who have never married. So the women are better equipped to compete in the job market but less likely to find parity when seeking a mate.[6]

Black women have all the same struggles as others, but they must also contend with two other social forces: racial bias among potential spouses of other races and the aftermath of America's war on drugs and its impacts on black men. One analysis of US Census data reported that black women were the least likely of all races to marry outside their race.[7] As recently as 2011, *Christianity Today* magazine reported that twice as many white evangelicals than Americans overall said interracial marriage would be bad for society. White Protestants and Catholics were not far behind.[8] As a result, black women immersed in multiracial and white Christian communities are far less likely to be married than their counterparts of other races.

A few years ago, I reconnected with a dear family friend from Philadelphia. We grew up in similar middle-class neighborhoods. Her parents were professionals like mine. I'd had a massive crush on her older brother, who looked just like Michael Jackson (back when MJ looked black). If her brother had asked me to be his girlfriend at any time during sixth grade, I would have fainted from the glee of it.

During our conversation, my friend, who also was still single, confided to me that her brother was in jail. Apparently, a traffic violation landed him behind bars. (I have no idea what type of traffic violation.) She is in regular contact with him, and during a phone call, he made a telling observation. "I used to wonder where all the black men in the neighborhood went. You know? They all just seemed to disappear—move away or something. But now that I'm in here, I see they're all in here. This place is full of black men."

The outcomes of America's drug wars on African American men were well documented by Michelle Alexander's groundbreaking book *The New Jim Crow in an Age of Colorblindness.* A 2014 analysis by the Brookings Institution reported, "An estimated one-third of black male Americans will spend time in state or federal prison at some point in their lifetime—more than double the rate from the 1970s and over five times higher than the rate for white males."[9] Meaningful employment, increased wages, and integration into civil society are blocked by incarceration. These barriers to social mobility for one-third of black men leave black women with fewer viable marriage options.[10]

One sliver of hope for black women comes from a February 2015 report posted on AtlantaBlackStar.com. According to their analysis of a 2010 US Census survey, black women are not doomed to never get married. Rather, they are likely to marry later. "The U.S. Census Bureau revealed that only thirteen percent of black women had never married by the age of 55." In fact, because of structural barriers to the economic advancement of black men, the article explained, many African American women are taking time to secure their own financial status before marrying. This means more education and more working years prior to marriage.[11]

BREAKING RELATIONSHIP THROUGH DIVORCE

The union of two who become one is a spiritual reality of marriage. Likewise, disunion holds spiritual weight, and divorce leaves broken and often dying families in its wake. Those affected face disillusionment, chaos, and confusion.

The common myth about US divorce rates is that 50 percent of marriages in the United States end in divorce and that the divorce rate is rising. That used to be true, but it's not so true anymore. Current generations are choosing to marry later in life or not get married at all, so divorce rates are falling. On the surface, this is good news, but a closer look at the numbers reveals that divorce is in decline only among more educated couples. The rates of divorce among couples with less education is nearing the peak levels reached in the 1970s. "As the middle of our labor market has eroded, the ability of high-school-educated Americans to build a firm economic foundation for a marriage has been greatly reduced," wrote Andrew Cherlin, a sociologist and author of *Labor's Love Lost: The Rise and Fall of the Working-Class Family in America*.[12] Less-educated Americans largely make up the working class and lower-middle class. For them, economic opportunity is greatly limited, leading to a loss of health and hope for many. As a result, they are divorcing at high rates or choosing to hold off on marrying until economic circumstances get better. All signs point to a long wait.

> To save his life, Abram persuaded his wife to lie.

The unavoidable effect of economic conditions on families dates to ancient times. Fleeing famine, Abram and Sarai went to Egypt. Because they were foreigners there, Abram was getting worried. He told Sarai, "Say you are my sister." Why?

Because it was widely understood that Pharaoh would take beautiful female immigrants into his harem and kill their husbands. To save his life, Abram persuaded his wife to lie.

Lest you see that as a mild infraction, remember that Paul listed liars among those for whom the Old Testament law was written. But Abram chose that path, and his life was spared. Sarai, meanwhile, was taken into the Pharaoh's harem. Bear in mind that women were added to the harem for sexual purposes. In other words, Sarai was raped. She was forced to have sex with a man who was not her husband. Abram gained favor for his brotherly relationship with Sarai and received land, animals, and male and female slaves; the female slaves likely had sexual relations with him. One lie separated their family, caused Sarai to suffer violation, and distorted the family structure to the point where it was no longer recognizable.

Then God's wrath was revealed, but not against Abram. God's wrath was centered on Pharaoh, whose selfish governance pushed Abram to lie. It was Pharaoh's public policy that disregarded the well-being of the poor and immigrants within his borders. "The LORD afflicted Pharaoh and his house with great plagues because of Sarai, Abram's wife" (Genesis 12:17), and God never said a word to rebuke Abram.

Ungodly governance—self-serving use of authority that seeks its own way to peace through policies that reap others' oppression and poverty— breaks families apart. We see how economic disparity impacts American families. We see it in the impact of mass incarceration, discussed earlier. And we see it in an examination of how today's broken immigration system affects immigrant families within our borders.

On November 12, 2013, in a white tarp tent on the National Mall, I sat in a circle with faith leaders and immigrants who had committed to fast and pray for immigration reform. Five of us fasted for twenty-two days. Each day, we came together in the tent and shared the life experiences that pushed us to fast. Within the first few days, I was overwhelmed by one truth: immigration reform is not about politics. It's not about Republicans and Democrats. It's about families.

One night a mother from Mexico sat in our circle and shared her story through a translator. She came to the United States years earlier in the midst of an economic depression in Mexico, caused in large part by American trade policy. America subsidized the cost of growing corn and then sold extremely cheap corn to Mexico, where the chief crop is corn. Mexican farmers couldn't compete with America's engineered prices, so farms went out of business throughout the country. Farmers moved to cities where the safety-net infrastructure already was weak. It didn't take long for the net to break, leaving mothers and fathers without a way to provide for their children.

And this is where US immigration policy could help, but most often it exacerbates the problems. Under current law there are only five thousand US work visas available to applicants from all countries each year. Only five hundred are allotted for Mexico. Our visitor, Maria, faced a twenty-year wait to get into the United States by legal means. Like Abram, she had a choice. She could remain in Mexico and watch her children suffer, or she could break the law and enter the United States, find work, and send money home to feed her children. She made the horrific trek through the desert, found work, and began sending money home.

Maria's voice began to tremble. "I miss my daughter," she said, weeping. "My original plan was to send for my children when I established myself here, but it's too dangerous now. I long for the day when I can see my children again."

One after another immigrant shared similar stories of family separation due either to the migrant experience or to loved ones having been detained during a routine traffic stop, thrown in jail, and deported.

Oppression rears its head in different forms in each generation, but in every instance it attacks families. It wasn't supposed to be this way.

Perhaps in a twist of irony, at the same time most American families are facing formidable social and structural challenges, the LGBTQ (Lesbian, Gay, Bisexual, Transgender, Queer) community is opting *into* the institution. Regardless of what one thinks of LGBTQ relationships, the US Supreme Court's five-to-four ruling in the case of *Obergefell v. Hodges* has legalized a new family structure across the country. Still, men, women, and transgendered people face the same separation from families and faith communities that they faced before the high court ruling. In my book *Forgive Us: Confessions of a Compromised Faith,* coauthored with Soong-Chan Rah, Mae Cannon, and Troy Jackson, we discerned that the single greatest sin of the church against LBGTQ people is the lack of recognition of the image of God within them. They are people with minds, hearts, stories, families, and dreams. Will Jesus followers rise above theoretical arguments and political wrangling to love their LGBTQ daughters, sons, mothers, fathers, aunties, uncles, and fellow parishioners? It is the lack of love—and the separation that results—that cuts deepest for many in the LGBTQ community.

FROM ALL OF US TO YOU AND YOURS

The kind of emptiness I felt during my mom's Christmas visit seems most powerful for people around the holiday season. Perhaps pushed by the depth of beauty in the season, humanity's deepest longings erupt. The soul's call for God's very goodness in our families is met by the stark reality of separation. Some families face down holidays in a state of shattered isolation. Other families put on a show of solidarity, with traditional foods and rituals that move time backward. But under the surface, the recurring failure to listen and care plus pride and a focus on self-protection build walls of separation between family members. Holidays clarify the depth of our longing for God's good news for broken families. We know in our bones that it wasn't supposed to be this way, but what is the hope in the midst of pain?

Abraham's grandson Jacob had twelve sons in a blended family—the sons of Leah and Rachel along with the sons of their maids. Jacob's son Joseph was the first son born to Rachel, who died while giving birth to Joseph's younger brother, Benjamin. Jacob loved Joseph. As a demonstration of his love, Jacob presented Joseph with a beautiful long robe that he had made (see Genesis 37:3). The only other mention of such a robe is the one Tamar wore, and it was a mark of royalty. In the case of Joseph, the robe was a special sign of sonship. As one of only two sons whose mother was not there to care for them, and living with ten stepbrothers and their mothers, one can imagine how Joseph craved extra attention from his father. Like Cain with Abel, Joseph's brothers resented the love their father had for Joseph. To make matters worse, Joseph started talking about his dreams that one day he would exercise dominion over his brothers. This caused his brothers to hate him all the more.

One day Joseph's brothers were working in a field when Jacob told Joseph to go fetch them. Jacob didn't realize that Joseph wasn't safe when alone with his brothers. Jacob was either in denial or so separated from the dynamics at play in his household that he was unaware that he had sent his beloved son into danger.

The text says the brothers saw Joseph from a distance and conspired to kill him. When he reached them, they stripped Joseph of his robe, ripping the status of sonship away from him and leaving him exposed. It is a shaming act. Remember that in Genesis 3, God made garments of animal skins to cover the shame of the man and woman. The brothers threw Joseph into a pit and were ready to leave him there for dead when Judah got the idea to save his life while making a tidy profit. They sold Joseph into slavery.

One moment he was headed to a field to get his brothers, the next he was beaten, betrayed, rejected, stripped of family ties, imprisoned, and trafficked. In Genesis 42:21, the brothers acknowledged the anguish they saw on Joseph's face as he pleaded with them not to sell him. But they didn't relent, and Joseph was taken in bondage far from his family. I imagine there were no words, only the pain of separation.

It's like that for us sometimes. Our families break and separation comes in and there's nothing we can do about it.

Over the two years after that Christmas spent with my mother, I gained fifty pounds. I threw myself into my work. I lived outside of myself, for everyone but me. In a constant state of moving from one thing to the next, detached from my own body, detached from the state of my wounded soul, I turned to food to cope. Food made it all feel better, until it didn't. The fifty pounds I gained made it harder to walk, travel, and climb steps. The weight gain was my failed attempt to cover over my shame rather than go to God.

What is it for you? Drugs, sex, television, adventure highs, work?

A friend recently asked me, "Where have you encountered God in all of it?"

That is the miracle of Joseph. The next mention of the brother sold into slavery picks up his story in Egypt: "The LORD was with Joseph" (Genesis

39:2). This phrase is repeated several times throughout the story of Joseph. The Lord was with Joseph when he was thrown into prison after being accused of raping Potiphar's wife. The Spirit of God was in Joseph when he interpreted Pharaoh's dreams and saved Egypt from suffering through seven years of famine. And here is the most amazing thing to me: though Joseph had been stripped of his father's robe, God moved Pharaoh to fill the gap in Joseph's soul. Pharaoh gave Joseph a signet ring, the equivalent of calling him a son. He gave him fine linens and garments. And he gave him a wife and a new name. Pharaoh placed Joseph second in command, like a son. As Joseph moved through the streets, the people called out in front of him, "Bow the knee."

In the middle of his pain, Joseph found God and found that God was enough. He simply walked forward. He walked with God, and God honored him.

There are mornings when I wake up and my first thought is of my estranged family. And I weep.

"Where have you encountered God in all of it?" my friend asked.

I have encountered God in my tears and in the surrogate family God brought into my life through long-lost cousins. I've encountered God in deep healing conversations with my mother and youngest sister. I've encountered God as I have watched my mother heal and reach for God and be met by God and begin to thrive. And I've encountered God through incredible experiences such as the Fast for Families, the people of Ferguson, Missouri, and the experience of living fully into God's dream for my life. The Lord has been with me.

But the story is not over. In an ironic twist, Joseph was reunited with his brothers when they came to Egypt to buy food during a famine. At first they didn't recognize him. Eventually, Joseph revealed himself, and in the next breath he exercised godly dominion over his family. It was the same kind of dominion we saw exercised in the Garden of Eden.

"I will provide for you (*kuwl,* to keep and maintain life)," Joseph said. With these words, Joseph answered Cain's question "Am I my brother's keeper?" The answer is yes.

Joseph, from his position in government, demonstrated that God wants to use faith-filled people to bless all of society, to feed the hungry, to house the homeless, to father the fatherless, to bless the prisoner, and to bless whole nations. "Yes," Joseph said, "we are our brothers' keepers."

Jesus, in the last sermon he preached on earth, broadened the category of who constitutes family. "I was hungry . . . , I was thirsty . . . , I was a stranger . . . , I was naked . . . , I was sick . . . , I was in prison," Jesus said. "Truly I tell you, just as you did it to one of the least of these *who are members of my family,* you did it to me" (Matthew 25:35–36, 40). The least are Jesus's family. It is impossible to love Jesus without loving the least of these within our families, within our churches and communities, within our cities,

> "Yes," Joseph said, "we are our brothers' keepers."

our states, our nation, and within our world. By loving the least of these, we honor and serve the image of God within all humanity.

God is committed to broken families. Whether it involves the interpersonal dynamics of domination or a systemic oppression that breaks families, God is committed to reconciling families. Sin is separation, and it always will be part of the experience of our fallen world. But the promise is this: in the middle of the pain—in the middle of the yawning divide in our families, in the middle of deepest longing for shalom in our closest relationships—God meets us. And God fills the gap through God's faithful people and through godly governance.

Reflection Exercise

1. Reflect on your family dynamics. In what ways are the dynamics most like the Genesis 1–2 picture of equal dominion? In which relationships do you experience protection, servanthood, and encouragement? In which relationships do you experience domination, jealousy, lack of communication, separation, and loss of hope?

2. Thank God for the healthy relationships in your family. (This includes your immediate family and other relatives.) Pray a prayer of blessing for those people and relationships. Ask God to meet you in the pain of broken relationships.

3. You cannot control the actions of others. You can control only your own words and actions. You can walk forward with the understanding that you are not alone. God is with you, and God is committed to you. God's ways offer a way to peace. Ask God to show you what it will look like for you to walk forward in God's ways.

4. If you are suffering physical, emotional, sexual, or mental violence within your family, call the National Domestic Violence Hotline for help at 1-800-799-SAFE (7233) or TTY 1-800-787-3224.

Finally, know that you are not alone. All families are broken on some level because we live in a fallen world. Sin and separation are guaranteed in this life. There is no shame in your family's situation; there is only an opportunity to experience more of God.

Shalom and Race

August 22, 2014. I pull my rental car into the parking lot of Three Kings Public House across the street from Washington University in St. Louis. I'm here to talk with evangelical faith leaders about what had happened twenty minutes away on August 9.

As he walked home from a convenience store in the suburb of Ferguson, eighteen-year-old Michael Brown was shot and killed by a Ferguson police officer. Brown's body lay in the middle of the street for four and a half hours. The officer involved, Darren Wilson, filed a nearly blank incident report. But the account given by police chief Jon Belmar conflicted with various eye-witness reports. Candlelight vigils turned violent. Young people from the area took to the streets in protest. The Ferguson Police Department brought out military-grade vehicles, equipment, and weapons in an effort to contain the protests. Tear-gas canisters were fired into the crowd. Demonstrators were ordered off the streets. News reporters were assaulted. The Missouri State Highway Patrol took over security, and after one night of quiet, violent clashes broke out again.

I followed the events on the news and didn't sleep for a week. A single question haunted me: With so many white and multiethnic evangelical churches in St. Louis, why weren't there more white people and other non-African American ethnicities marching with the people of Ferguson?

I landed in St. Louis on Wednesday, August 20, with one primary goal: to help build a bridge between white and multiethnic churches and the movement for justice in Ferguson. Two days later, I ended a call with my boss, Jim Wallis, and walked into Three Kings pub. It was time to show the people of Ferguson they were not alone.

Howie Meloch, the associate regional director of a college ministry in the area, greeted me at the door. He had assembled a number of top white, black, and Asian American leaders of evangelical churches, networks, and ministries in St. Louis. Leroy Barber, author of *Red, Brown, Yellow, Black, White—Who's More Precious in God's Sight?*, co-facilitated the gathering.

I spoke about the Genesis 1:26–27 declaration that all humanity is made in the image of God and emphasized that in the same breath, God said he would give humanity dominion. I reflected on four implications of that truth:

1. Every person in this restaurant, every person on the street, and every person in Ferguson is made in the image of God.

2. That means that, all things being equal, every person was created with the command and the capacity to exercise the Genesis 1:26–27 dominion, which means to steward or, in modern terms, to exercise agency or to lead.

3. To diminish or ignore the ability of humans to exercise dominion is to diminish or ignore the image of God in them. And it is to diminish or ignore God's image on earth.

4. The fastest and surest way to diminish the ability of humans to exercise agency is through poverty and/or oppression.

Leroy Barber reflected on Isaiah 61:1–5, reminding us that Isaiah said there is one who will proclaim good news to the oppressed. He pointed out that Jesus quoted this passage in his first sermon on earth. He reminded us of the prophecy in verses 3–4: "They will be called oaks of righteousness. . . . They shall build up the ancient ruins, they shall raise up the former devastations; they shall repair the ruined cities, the devastations of many generations." Leroy mentioned that those who would take action are oppressed, brokenhearted captives and prisoners, the ones who mourn. It is a description of the people of Ferguson.

I called the pastors and other leaders to a time of reflection. Here's the question: "Do you believe this? How does it make you feel in your gut to imagine being led to peace by the people of Ferguson?"

In the discussion that followed, one forty-something leader stood, shifting his weight from left to right. Then he leaned against a wall, as if asking it to hold him up. He looked at me, as if asking permission to speak. I nodded. Then he stood straight and spoke.

"As a white man," he said, "I have been taught I was created to lead everyone else."

Another St. Louis faith leader confessed, "It never even occurred to me that I would be led by the people of Ferguson. It never entered my mind as a possibility."

We have believed a lie whose roots run deep in Western thought. It has shaped Western worldview, structures, legal paradigms, and the church. To glimpse the way to shalom in the arena of race, we must first understand the dimensions and outcomes of this lie. To do that we must clarify terms and understand how they intersect with or contradict biblical teaching.

Ethnicity, Culture, Nationality, and the Tower of Babel

Race, ethnicity, culture, and *nationality* often are used as interchangeable words, but each one has a different shade of meaning. They have different origins, purposes, and outcomes. And in truth, there is no universally accepted definition for any of these terms. What I'm going to share are the ways I've come to understand them after training and teaching on justice and racial healing for twenty years.

Ethnicity is biblical (Hebrew: *goy* or *am;* Greek: *ethnos*). Ethnicity is created by God as people groups move together through space and time. Ethnicity is dynamic and developed over long periods of time. It is not about power. It is about group identity, heritage, language, place, and common group experience over time. Ethnicity is the difference between African American, Caribbean, British African, Irish, Irish American, Korean, Korean American, English, Anglo-American, Polish, Polish American, and so forth. Ethnicity is God's very good intention for humanity.

> Ethnicity is God's very good intention for humanity.

Culture is implicit in Scripture, but the word itself is never used. Culture is a sociological and anthropological term that refers to the beliefs, norms, rituals, arts, and worldviews of particular people groups in a particular place at a particular time. Culture is fluid.

Nationality indicates the sovereign nation/state where an individual is a legal citizen. It is a geopolitical category determined by the legal structures of the state. I tend to think the best indicator of nationality is the birth certificate or passport the individual holds.

Many English translations of the Bible translate the Hebrew and Greek words for ethnicity as "nation," but we must understand that nation-states the way that we understand them, as territorially and politically drawn areas of geography with a shared government, did not exist prior to the late eighteenth century. Nation-states are a modern construct. Before the modern era, people organized themselves around ethnic tribes, clans, and ethnically based empires.

THE TOWER OF BABEL

The first uses of the Hebrew word *goy* (foreign ethnic group) in Genesis are instructive. The word is found in the list of Noah's descendants, commonly called the Table of Nations (see Genesis 10). The word is found next in the story of the Tower of Babel (see Genesis 11). Most scholars now understand that the same company of priests that wrote Genesis 1 also wrote the Table of Nations in chapter 10, while the writer of Genesis 2 also wrote Genesis 11. In the same way that Genesis 1 offers a sweeping account of creation and Genesis 2 offers a more detailed and separate account, the Table of Nations offers a sweeping foretelling of the fulfillment of the mandate to multiply and fill the earth and the Tower of Babel story offers a more specific and separate account of how the mandate was fulfilled.

Before the Tower of Babel was destroyed, "the whole earth had one language and the same words" (Genesis 11:1). The people gathered there had come from the east to the land of Shinar, where they settled. Shinar exhibits the major characteristics of empire: a single trade language and a commitment to erecting tall buildings and monuments despite the oppression and exploitation of slave labor.

The enslaved laborers were working with materials—brick and

bitumen—that are dangerous when erecting such a large structure. Brick is man-made and it crumbles over time. Bitumen, similar to tar, is an asphalt-like substance used to hold the bricks together, something like mortar or cement. A survey of monuments that have lasted throughout the ages confirms that structures built using stone on stone are the sturdiest and longest lasting. A structure of brick and bitumen eventually will crumble. It is an unstable construction method. In an act of care for human life, God intervened by confusing the people's language. Jehovah scattered them lest they bring great destruction on more and more people.

More than any other, this text lays the foundations for understanding God's good intentions for shalom, ethnicity, and culture. Walter Brueggemann explains in his commentary *Genesis: Interpretation: A Bible Commentary for Teaching and Preaching* that the scattering of the peoples was not a curse, as some have interpreted it. It was a blessing.[1]

As they were scattered, the people would settle in a wider area, having the chance to fulfill the basic human call to multiply and fill the earth. They would develop separate languages, cultures, and worldviews. And each group would experience distinct trials and triumphs and develop core strengths and weaknesses as a result. Their various ethnic heritages would be forged through common experiences of life together. According to Brueggemann, God's kind of unity will be achieved as all parts of the diverse human family "look to and respond to God" from their respective corners of the world.[2]

As counterintuitive as it sounds, the confusion of languages was from God. Like the Tree of the Knowledge of Good and Evil in Genesis 2, the reality that humanity speaks a multiplicity of languages cannot be dealt with successfully without God. Like the Tree of the Knowledge of Good and Evil, the confusion of languages serves as a reminder of our limitations. It draws us back to God, beckoning us to find shalom between ethnic groups in and through God.

THE WAY OF GOD

In the person of Jesus, we see God incarnate crossing the ethnic boundaries of his day. He conversed with the Samaritan woman, the demoniac, the Syrophoenician woman, and the Roman centurion. On the cross, the tablet above Jesus's head—King of the Jews—was written in several languages as a taunt, mocking a supposed king. But the tablet actually made it possible for Jesus to cross ethnic and lingual barriers even in death.

When the Holy Spirit was released among God's people (see Acts 2: 1–13), the confusion of languages at the Tower of Babel was reversed. Men and women who did not share a common language were suddenly speaking and understanding unfamiliar languages. God was indicting imperial rule, which demands the exclusion of ethnic identity to consolidate a dominant culture. Instead, the Spirit of God maintained lingual and thus cultural and ethnic diversity while at the same time making it possible for disparate groups to understand one another. Paul pointed to Jesus's power to reconcile Jews and Gentiles, bitter ethnic enemies, as an example of the power of the Resurrection. "For he is our peace; in his flesh he has made both groups into one and has broken down the dividing wall, that is, the hostility between us" (Ephesians 2:14).

In the Temple, a wall separated the Gentile court from the Jews. A written warning told Gentiles not to cross beyond that point upon the pain of death. That's hostility.

But Jesus broke down that wall. When he beat death, he began the reversal of the Fall. Having overcome the one power that all humanity must encounter, he ensured he could beat all other powers of division and separation, including the power of ethnic enmity.

What might our churches look like if we believed and practiced this? What dividing walls of hostility would fall? What policies and structures would be transformed? How might our desire to be safe—keeping ethnically and culturally insulated, protected from critique, challenge, and change—be transformed by encounters with the living God? How much more of Jesus would people of faith experience if they allowed him to break down walls of ethnic and cultural difference?

Dr. Martin Luther King Jr. said, "Eleven o'clock on Sunday morning is one of the most segregated hours—if not the most segregated hour—in Christian America." Perhaps churches have committed themselves to building and maintaining Towers of Babel. Towers of Babel require efficiency, uniformity, a single language, and a dominant culture. They are enemies of the image of God on earth, yet the church continues to study the Tower of Babel user manual so it can build bigger, brighter, more efficient monuments. I believe that the call of God to the church in these days is to dismantle Babel. Return to worshiping communities rooted in place, where power is shared. In such places, the image of God and the capacity to exercise dominion in all cultures and languages are affirmed and cultivated.

METRO HOPE

Tucked in the northeast corner of gentrifying Spanish Harlem, in Upper Manhattan, Metro Hope Church was founded in 2007. It is a diverse congregation with ninety worshipers on a good Sunday, and it is surrounded by historic black megachurches, Hispanic megachurches, and affluent white church plants. The church plants are commissioned by white megachurches with the goal of ministering to the needy who live above 125th Street—or to minister to those who migrate there to gentrify the area.

New York City is incredibly diverse while also achieving in 2011 the rank of second-most-segregated city in a study conducted by CensusScope.org and the University of Michigan.[3] While most New York churches cater to single ethnic groups, Metro Hope is roughly 40 percent African American, 35 percent Latino, 20 percent White, and 5 percent Asian/Pacific Islander.

Reverend José Humphreys, an Afro-Puerto Rican pastor in the area, leads his faith community through the "mindful practice of seeing one another through the eyes of Christ." Sunday morning worship is infused with Harlem's jazz fusion spirit. I visited the church soon after a Staten Island grand jury decided not to indict the police officer who killed Eric Garner. The congregation's white associate pastor, Stephen Tickner, preached the sermon and moved directly into the fray of public policy and the biblical call to justice. In fact, Tickner, Humphreys, and others on Metro Hope's leadership team were among the leaders who organized faith communities to join the massive protest marches that shut down the West Side Highway in Manhattan the night the decision not to indict was announced.

During the week, the Metro Hope community's leadership team might host a transformative group dialogue on an issue of race, ethnicity, culture, or justice; sponsor an event to harvest the church's community garden; hang out at a local coffee shop to help support indigenous businesses; or start dialogue among the members of the church's intentional living community.

To Metro Hope, subverting Babel looks like planting seeds of shalom in the lives of its parishioners through radical community, hospitality, and commitment to the personal, social, economic, and cultural flourishing of their city.[4]

That brings us to race.

RACE, DOMINION, AND THE IMAGE OF GOD

Race is about power—in biblical terms, *dominion*. As a political construct, race was created by humans to determine who can exercise power within a governing structure and to guide decisions regarding how to allocate resources. Racial categories do change over time, but only as governments refine language.

Plato's *The Republic* (360 BCE) laid the foundations for the Western belief in human hierarchy. According to Plato, God created a class hierarchy determined by "racial" categories delineated by the kind of metal people were made of: gold, silver, iron, or brass. Each "race" was ordained to hold different stations in society. Book VIII laid the foundations for the belief that the mixing of the races would lead to destruction.[5]

Fast-forward to 1452. Pope Nicholas V paved the way for the Portuguese slave trade in West Africa when he authorized Alfonzo V of Portugal to perpetually enslave anyone not Christian, especially Muslims. Three years later, the same pope issued the papal bull *Romanus Pontifex,* declaring that Catholic nations had the right to "discover" and claim dominion over non-Christian lands. The bull also encouraged the enslavement of the indigenous peoples of conquered lands.[6]

Fast-forward to the Enlightenment era. In 1767, Swedish botanist Carl

Linnaeus, founder of botany's taxonomy of fauna, published the twelfth edition of his *Systema Naturae,* which defined the first taxonomy of human racial hierarchy based on skin color.

Twenty years later, the US Congress made official what the courts of the American colonies had already established by precedent. The newly formed United States of America enacted the racialization of power. Congress passed the three-fifths compromise, which increased the number of members in the House of Representatives who represented districts in the slave states. Congress determined that each enslaved person would be counted as three-fifths of a human being. Congress members from the North had argued that slaves should not be factored into the populations of slave states. With the compromise, however, Congress declared that black people would be counted, but as less than human.

Three years later Northerners got their way on the first national census in 1790. Enslaved black people were listed as chattel—nonhuman property—along with pitchforks and horses.

In the same year, Congress passed the Naturalization Act of 1790, which declared that only free white men could become naturalized citizens. This was significant because only citizens can vote, and voting is the most basic form of the exercise of dominion. Other forms of dominion, such as the capacity to steward, to exercise agency, and to lead, hinge on this basic right. With this law in place, for the next century new immigrants to the United States could be legally categorized as white.

In 1922, the US Supreme Court heard the case of Mr. Takao Ozawa, a Japanese man who argued that Japanese people are white. Ozawa had been in the country for twenty years and wanted to become naturalized. He had been blocked by the Naturalization Act of 1906, which restricted naturalization to free white people and people of African descent. The court denied Ozawa's claim to whiteness and, with it, his chances of becoming a citizen.

We see our nation's struggle to define race in changing categories used when a national census is conducted. In the first US census in 1790, racial categories included free white, free other, and slave. Thirty years later, racial categories were expanded to include free colored and foreigners (not naturalized). And every ten years following 1830, our country has struggled to adjust its racial categories to match the growing complexity of our people groups. By 2010, the census revealed the absurdity of the fundamental category of race. In that census, race, ethnicity, and nationality were combined into a single category of race.[7] The 1850 census took place at the height of the American slave trade and in the midst of the Second Great Awakening, which called slave masters to free their slaves. The census that year sought to capture the realities of an increasingly complex human landscape. According to a report on Census.gov, the 1850 Free Inhabitants schedule listed races as white, black, or mulatto (mixed). The schedule had a separate question regarding place of origin, and there was a completely separate schedule for slaves. The slave schedule delineated race using two categories, black or mulatto. Chinese men from Canton Province began arriving in the United States to work for the Central Pacific Railroad in 1850. By 1868, twelve thousand Chinese men worked for the company. The 1870 census responded by adding Chinese to the list of races. The category incorporated all people of Eastern descent. In this year, the census incorporated the category Indian for Native American but only counted assimilated peoples living in or near white communities. In 1890, eight years after the Chinese Exclusion Act (1882), the census delineated between Chinese and Japanese. It also attempted to capture the complexity of mixed-race heritage by adding quadroon and octoroon to the list of races. A review of the 2010 census shows the categories Hispanic, Latino, and Spanish ethnic origin, with an option to write in one's nation of origin. The census lists "racial" categories, and respondents choose one or more categories, which were white, "black, African am., or Negro," "American Indian or Alaska Native—*Print name of enrolled or principal tribe*," Asian Indian, Chinese, Filipino, Japanese, Korean, Vietnamese, "Other Asian—*Print race, for example Hmong, Laotian, Thai, Pakistani, Cambodian, and so on*," Native Hawaiian, Guamanian or Chamorro, Samoan, "Other Pacific Islander—*Print race, for example, Fijian, Tongan, and so on*," "Some other race—*Print race.*"

Why does the federal government ask for the nations of origin for Asian and Latino people, tribal affiliation for American Indian people, and include "African American" (a specific ethnic group within the racial category "black") but does not ask "white" people to identify their ethnicity or nation of origin?

It's because of power. The only racial category on the national census that did not change from 1790 to 2010 was "white." In the United States, whiteness is the centerpiece around which all else revolves. That was and is intentional. In 1751, Benjamin Franklin argued to the British ministry that due to the shrinking percentage of white people on earth, America should be kept an exclusively Anglo-Saxon colony to protect the race.[8] In the years following the establishment of our nation, the founders followed Franklin's lead and white

> In the United States, whiteness is the centerpiece around which all else revolves.

became the identity of power.[9] Race is inherently about power, and whiteness was created to define who would wield it.

The core lie of Western civilization is that God reserved the power of dominion for some, not all. Since the Enlightenment era, that lie has been racialized. With the founding of our nation, racialized dominion was made law with one resounding message: God reserved the right of dominion for white people and no one else.

IMPLICIT BIAS

Across the centuries, the image of God has been breached throughout the world. The breach is the result of what psychologists call explicit (conscious) and implicit (unconscious) ethnic bias. Explicit bias laid foundations for the international slave trade, the annihilation of indigenous peoples on every continent, and the establishment of racial hierarchy. Explicit bias built the systems we continue to operate under in America. Implicit (unconscious) racial bias, meanwhile, looks at our broken world and says, "Things are as they should be." Implicit bias is what the mind does when it makes quick associations in order to shorten its thought processes. For example, when encountering a table, the mind does not say *It has four legs and a plank, therefore it is a table.* It just looks at the object and immediately associates it with *table.* Unconscious association is a normal part of brain functionality. But in our racialized society, we have learned to make unconscious associations with whiteness and blackness and other people of color.

The study of implicit racial bias has revealed deep-seated beliefs about people of European descent and African descent. Millions of people have taken the Implicit Association Test, created by Project Implicit, a collaboration between scientists at Harvard, the University of Virginia, and the University of Washington, to discern their levels of implicit bias. Seventy-five percent of respondents have tested positive for some level of bias in favor of whiteness and against blackness. That means 75 percent of people tested associate factors such as goodness, high leadership capacity, benevolence, truthfulness, high financial standing, and lack of criminality with people who look like they are of European descent. Conversely, 75 percent associate things such as badness, low leadership capacity, lack of character, poverty, and criminality with people who look like they are of black African descent. What was most notable was that respondents across various races and ethnicities had the same implicit biases. It also didn't matter if they had dedicated their lives to fighting racism and injustice. Seventy-five percent of *all* respondents tested positive for implicit bias in favor of whiteness.[10]

The Kirwan Institute for the Study of Race and Ethnicity at Ohio State University discovered that implicit bias impacts every level of the justice system, from first encounters with police to the decision whether to arrest, shoot, or release a detained person. Implicit bias impacts the booking process, the quality and content of legal defense, judge selection, a jury's perceptions of the defendant, and sentencing. The Kirwan study also found that implicit bias impacts the way teachers treat students, the way properties are valued—impacting school funding—and even the way health care functions.[11]

From Plato to mass incarceration, the belief that certain people were created to rule and others were created to be ruled has been so deeply ingrained in our collective worldview that we don't question these disparities. Implicit bias tells us things are as they should be. Unjust systems and structures remain in place because the people do not demand a better world.

But that is not what God has called us to.

Baptism

In his letter to the Galatians, Paul wrote, "As many of you as were baptized into Christ have clothed yourselves with Christ. There is no longer Jew or Greek, there is no longer slave or free, there is no longer male or female; for all of you are one in Christ Jesus" (3:27–28). These words became the first baptismal liturgy of the church. Baptism, as a result, connected the outward demonstration of washing clean to the inner cleansing of all implicit and explicit biases that were entrenched within the systems and structures of both Roman and Jewish society.

Roman imperial systems and structures were built in part on Plato's belief in human hierarchy. But Christian baptism, from the start, erased the power differentials. This celebration of Christ's death and resurrection reminds us to see, protect, and cultivate the image of God in the other—to recognize and cultivate the other's capacity to exercise dominion. This was radical teaching in Paul's day. It remains so today.

Washing Clean

What does it look like to be washed clean of twenty-first-century implicit bias? Here are practices that research has shown help cleanse people of implicit racial bias.

Become Aware

Take the Implicit Association Test at https://implicit.harvard.edu/implicit/education.html (or Google "Implicit Association Test") and choose the Race IAT (Race Implicit Association Test). This test measures how hard we have to work to undo the associations the test puts into our subconscious. Not having to work that hard indicates the bias wasn't as strong to begin with. If it takes longer, then the participant started out with a stronger bias.

Grow Your Empathy

Listen to the stories of people who do not share your ethnicity. Read books and articles written by them. Watch movies by them and about them. The practice of placing ourselves in the shoes of others lowers the presence of unconscious bias.

Immerse Yourself

Increase and deepen relationships with people who do not share your ethnicity. When people build relationships with people they previously were biased against, their unconscious bias levels go down. In their book *Divided by Faith: Evangelical Religion and the Problem of Race in America*, Michael Emerson and Christian Smith reported on a sociological study they conducted. They found that the only way worldviews changed was for an individual to be immersed in communities populated by people the individual had been biased against.[12]

Take Every Thought Captive

Paul talked about taking every thought captive to gain the mind of Christ. This also works to lower implicit-bias scores. Researchers refer to it as changing habits of mind. They recommend that we focus on a person's unique traits as opposed to his or her group affiliation. I've been practicing something like this for the past year. When I'm talking with someone and am tempted to write the person off as "just a [fill in the blank]," I look the person in the eyes (if I can) and remember that the image of God lives inside the person. Then I sit in that truth. Suddenly, the person becomes fully human to me, with stories, histories, dreams, struggles, joys, and strengths.

Forsake Race

It is impossible to live justly within a manufactured system that was built with the purpose of defining who has power and who doesn't. That system runs counter to the ways of God. What would it look like for white Jesus followers to renounce their racial affiliation, to no longer accept the power and privilege allotted through the current system? Or to leverage it for the sake of others? And what kind of new world could we build if all of us on American soil—*all* of us—replaced race with our ethnic heritage (*ethnos*) rooted in place, language, and community? We would remember the history, study the ways race broke our world, and build the future that corrects its impacts. We would refuse to be defined by a lie. Then, perhaps, we would experience more of the power of the Resurrection as we brought our whole selves and the living power of the Resurrection into multiethnic community with our neighbors, in our schools, in our hospitals, in our courts, and in the public square.

BLACK LIVES MATTER

The Black Lives Matter movement exploded after the 2014 death of Michael Brown in Ferguson, Missouri. The movement was born as a hashtag in 2013. Three queer and cisgender black women crafted it in response to the acquittal of George Zimmerman for the death of Trayvon Martin. The #BlackLivesMatter movement spread like wildfire as reports of police killings of unarmed black men, women, and children appeared on news outlets almost daily. As of late 2015, the *Washington Post* recorded ninety police killings of unarmed people in just that one year. As mentioned earlier, thirty-five of the victims (40 percent) were black men, though black men make up only 6 percent of the US population. The Black Lives Matter movement is led by young black people because they are the ones most likely to face down a police officer aiming a gun. While the Black Lives Matter movement is secular in origin, I find its organizing principles quite biblical.

Isaiah 61: Oaks of Righteousness. The first organizing principle is that young black people must always be up-front, leading any Black Lives Matter initiative. This falls in line with the prophet Isaiah's admonition, "They will be called oaks of righteousness, the planting of the LORD, to display his glory. They shall build up the ancient ruins, they shall raise up the former devastations; they shall repair the ruined cities, the devastations of many generations" (61:3–4). Isaiah was referring to the oppressed, the brokenhearted, the captives, and the prisoners. They will restore and repair the ruins.

Matthew 25: The Least of These. If you watch newsreels reporting on the marches of the civil rights era, most show black people dressed in their Sunday best to march down the street. Men wore suits; women wore white gloves and heels to march on blistering asphalt. Rosa Parks was chosen to sit down in the white section of a city bus as an act of nonviolent civil disobedience in Montgomery, Alabama. She was chosen, in large part, because she was so "respectable" in the eyes of white people. She was an unassuming, light-skinned maid from a working-class family. This tactic worked in its time. People were appalled when they saw this respectable maid being booked by the Montgomery police. Likewise, the nation was aghast when they witnessed the brutality of Alabama state troopers who beat protestors on Selma's Edmund Pettus Bridge in 1965. The politics of respectability turned the nation's sympathy toward black people by humanizing them in the eyes of white people.

The problem was that the benefits of the civil rights movement were largely enjoyed by only the most respectable among black people—the black middle class. By and large, poor black people were shut out of the gains and suffered the brunt of America's war on drugs and mass incarceration. In response, a central organizing principle of Black Lives Matter organizers is to forsake the politics of respectability. Jesus identified with the least among us, and unless we are actively loving the one with the least access to food and water, the least access to health care, the least access to good housing and education, the least access to justice within the justice system, the least access to a welcome in the immigration system—unless we are actively loving the least-deserving among these, then we are not loving Jesus. Jesus shunned the politics of respectability when he aligned with the least of these.

Genesis 1:26–27: Dominion. What does it look like to become an accomplice in the Black Lives Matter movement? It looks like being submerged in the cleansing waters of Christ and rising with new eyes able to see. It means being ready to fan the flames of the image of God within young black leaders and other leaders of color. It looks like believing they are made in the image of God, made with the inherent call and capacity to exercise dominion. Young leaders of color are capable of leading us all into a better world. For white people this will mean entering the movement as learners, allies, or accomplices who leverage the privilege and resources they have for the building up of the movement. For people of color, this will mean rising up and leaning into their God-given call to lead us all to a better world. It will mean learning all they can from books and gleaning what they can from the elders. It will mean addressing and seeking their own healing from the deep wounds of oppression. And it will mean stewarding the well-being of all. For clergy and other faith leaders, it will mean offering ourselves as chaplains, foot soldiers, safe havens, and resources of the movement for a better world.

REPAIR

The institution of race broke America at its foundations. It will not be enough to tinker here and there. We need to envision a new way of being together. Fundamentally, this will mean the interrogation of all our assumptions about how our society should be. It will mean imagining a world where everyone—especially the least of these—has enough to thrive. It will mean a world where all at least have good enough education, good enough housing, good enough health care, good enough access to justice in the justice system, good enough protection of the right to vote, and good enough welcome to feel the embrace of the nation in order to thrive here. To find the folks working toward repair in your town, city, or state, do a Google search. Search a category—such as housing, education, employment, voting rights—plus the word *organizing* or *equity* plus the name of your town, city, or state. For example, "Education Equity Minneapolis." Click and a list of groups moving policies toward a more just education system will pop up. Search "Environmental Justice Organizing New York City" and a long list of groups will pop up. Once you do the search, show up. Once you show up, follow the lead of the people who are already there. That's how you become an ally/accomplice to the movement to repair what race broke. Here's an easy way to remember it: *Search. Find. Show Up. Follow.*

Reflection Exercise

Let's close with the reflection exercise that I led faith leaders through in St. Louis.

1. Close your eyes.
2. Remember Isaiah's statement that it will be the oppressed, the brokenhearted, the captives, and the imprisoned who will repair the ruined cities and the devastations of many generations.
3. Imagine yourself being led by the oppressed in your town, city, and state.
4. How does it feel in your gut to imagine following the lead of the least of these?
5. Be brutally honest with yourself. Do you believe the Scripture?
6. If not, then confess your unbelief to God, and ask God to help you believe. Then work through the "Washing Clean" section in this chapter.
7. If you believe, then ask God to guide your steps as you enter the movement to repair what race broke in America.

Shalom Between Nations

Gravel crunched beneath my feet with each step as if I were walking on dry bones. The sky was a dull, thick gray, an impenetrable blanket holding the memories of cries, prayers, and suffering to the cracked earth. I had just walked the same path that new arrivals at the Dachau concentration camp would have walked sixty years earlier.

In the summer of 2004, I was part of an international pilgrimage with twenty-five college students and ministry partners. Our goal was to learn from the people who had lived through the Balkan Wars a decade earlier. We wanted to know what they had come to understand about how shalom is broken and how it is rebuilt between nations. Dachau, Germany, was our first stop because the Croatian War of Independence (1991–1995) was fueled in part by the historical memory of Croatia's alliance with Hitler during World War II. The United States Holocaust Memorial Museum estimates the Croatian Ustaše regime killed as many as 340,000 ethnic Serbs from Croatia and Bosnia in Croatian concentration camps between 1941 and 1945.[1]

Dachau is the town where the first Nazi concentration camp was established. Originally built to house political prisoners, the camp remains standing in the sleepy town just ten miles outside Munich. I entered the main hall, where stark-naked people once stood with clothes in hand, waiting to be registered by SS men. This is where men and women lost their hair and their human identity and became a number. I walked forward to the baths—the shower room where these "numbers" were tortured. Their hands were tied behind their backs, and chains hoisted their arms up to bear the full weight of their bodies. Mangled images of God sagged there naked to amuse their captors.

The illusion of bones crunching under my feet would not abate. With each step I took, dust rose like powder, covering my flip-flopped feet, until I stood still in the roll-call courtyard. Upon this earth, men and women garbed in prisoners' black-and-white-striped rags once stood at attention for three or four hours at a time while tens of thousands of malnourished bodies were counted, given work assignments, and counted again at the end of each day. I looked at the trees and thought, *You were witnesses.*

Two reconstructed barracks told the story of the Holocaust's growth. The original camp was designed to hold six thousand prisoners. The first barrack was a reconstruction of that early period. Spacious wooden bunks stacked three tiers high filled the quarters. There were no mattresses, just bare planks for bedding. The second barrack, representing the later period, held more bunks, stacked four high with far less space per bunk. Several people were shoved into each of these disease-infested, hunger-riddled cubby holes. On the day of liberation, April 29, 1945, US troops found more than thirty thousand living skeletons in the camp.[2]

I walked to the crematorium and my heart started racing. I was also walking toward the place where, in Dachau's final years, the camp became a death camp. Determined to destroy all evidence of their genocide, the Nazis attempted to kill and burn as many prisoners as possible. Thirty-two thousand deaths were documented and thousands more went undocumented at Dachau. From 1933 to 1945, two hundred thousand Catholics, Protestants, Jews, Orthodox, Germans, Poles, Romany, Bavarians, peasants and princesses, artists, lawyers, doctors, scientists, mothers, fathers, daughters, sons, and grandparents—they all moved and breathed behind Dachau's electrified, barbed-wire fence. They all lived under the eyes of armed guards stationed in high towers simply because of who they were.

Dachau was an instrument of empire, the human compulsion to grow the bounds of the state's rule and to exercise that rule through domination, exploitation, and control. Hitler and the SS were carrying out the dreams of forefathers who had tried to dominate other European nations throughout the nineteenth and early twentieth centuries. Empire had been Germany's dream for nearly a century. The dream was fueled by centuries of examples of imperial regimes that sought to dominate other countries in an effort to ensure their own flourishing.

THE KIN-DOM OF GOD

As we discussed in the previous chapter, the Tower of Babel was an early attempt to build empire. The biblical narrative then leaps past generations and zeroes in on Abram, a descendent of Shem, who was a son of Noah. Abram is called to leave his people and go "to the land that I will show you" (Genesis 12:1).

This is a radical call for someone who likely lived in an agrarian society, where one's power and livelihood came from the acquisition of land. God's call to Abram was a call to downward mobility, not empire. It was a call to exercise faith, to uproot himself from that which brings stability and power, and to place himself and his family in the trustworthy hands of God. In return for his faith, God promised Abram, "I will make of you a great nation, and I will bless you, and make your name great, so that you will be a blessing" (verse 2). In a world where people groups were struggling to make names for themselves to increase their own power, God called Abram apart. God would make Abram's name great in order to bless others. In the story of Abram, we see the first seeds of God's intent to counter the oppressive empires of men with God's radical alternative, the kin-dom of God.

We have already seen God disperse the people of Shinar because their imperial building projects oppressed their own people and countered God's purpose to fill the earth. Now we see that the seed of God's intent was a radical new people group that would come through the seed of Abram—the seed of faith. Its purpose was clear: "In you all the families of the earth shall be blessed" (verse 3). The purpose of greatness is to bless, not oppress. And the blessing is for all the families of the earth.

Egypt was a place to which people commonly fled to escape famine and drought. One commentator has explained that unlike Canaan, Egypt had the Nile to keep its cropland fertile independent of seasonal rainfall.[3] In spite of Egypt's openness to asylum seekers, its Pharaoh leveraged power for his own pleasure, not the well-being of families seeking shelter in his land. In modern terms, Pharaoh used his men to prey on desperate women in their time of greatest need. Thus, soon after receiving the divine promise of greatness,

> The purpose of greatness is to bless, not oppress.

Abram and Sarai experienced one of the hallmarks of human empire: the impulse to exploit the other for selfish gain (see Genesis 12:10–20). By the end of Genesis 12, empire is on a collision course with God's shalom. Two chapters later, we see empire in full bloom:

> In the days of King Amraphel of Shinar [Babylon], King Arioch of Ellasar, King Chedorlaomer of Elam, and King Tidal of Goiim, these kings made war with King Bera of Sodom, King Birsha of Gomorrah, King Shinab of Admah, King Shemeber of Zeboiim, and the king of Bela (that is, Zoar). All these joined forces in the Valley of Siddim (that is, the Dead Sea). Twelve years they had served Chedorlaomer, but in the thirteenth year they rebelled.
> (Genesis 14:1–4)

The scene opens with a battle that commentators believe happened around 2084 BCE.[4] Five kings whose kingdoms had been colonized rose up and declared a war of independence against the imperial rule of King Chedorlaomer, ruler of Elam. Chedorlaomer responded by assembling a coalition of four eastern kings (including himself) to temper the uprising. Here, in the first verse of Genesis 14, we find the first mention of the word *king* in Genesis. In the same breath is the first mention of the word *war* (see verse 2). These words appear for the first time in the context of a struggle against empire. It took only fourteen chapters for the state of God's creation to shift from *tov me'od* ("very good") to war and empire.

Abram was tangentially swept up in this battle as he attempted to rescue his nephew, Lot, who was captured in the mayhem. King Chedorlaomer eventually was defeated, and the narrative returns to God's covenant

with Abram and the foundations laid for its fulfillment through the patriarchs of Israel. In the third generation after Abram, Joseph was trafficked to
Egypt. Egypt had not yet achieved the status of a political and military
empire, but through Joseph's experience, we see the growth of the imperial
impulse in Egypt. At the time of Abram, Pharaoh was exploiting individuals for personal gain. By Joseph's time, about 186 years later, human trafficking had become so common that Potiphar, the captain of this Pharaoh's
guard, was able to buy Joseph without a question being raised. Eventually,
Joseph's faith gained him influence with the Pharaoh and enabled him to
leverage the power of Pharaoh to bless the surrounding nations. At the con-
clusion of Joseph's narrative, the twelve tribes of Israel are listed. They are
descendants of Abraham and the next stage in fulfilling God's promise.
Joseph died reminding his brothers of God's promise: "God will surely
come to you, and bring you up out of this land to the land that he swore to
Abraham, to Isaac, and to Jacob" (Genesis 50:24).

Three hundred years after the death of Joseph, Egypt had become an
empire[5] The Israelites had multiplied and prospered in Egypt (see Exodus
1:7), but a new Pharaoh, who was unfamiliar with Joseph, blamed the pros-
perity of the Jews for the Egyptians' decline in power (see Exodus 1:8–9).
This Pharaoh enslaved the twelve tribes of Israel and put them to work
building supply cities for the empire. The sin had snowballed further. We
see in Exodus 1 the calculated development of ethnically based slavery.

God heard the cries of the enslaved Israelites. God answered the power
of human empire with the force of the Creator of heaven and earth. Moses
did as God told him, declaring to Pharaoh, "Let my people go" (Exodus 5:1;
9:1). Pharaoh repeatedly refused to listen, so each time Creator God moved
creation with greater force. The God over the deep turned the Nile into a

river of blood. The God who made frogs, gnats, and flies called them to take over. The God who created horses, donkeys, camels, herds, and flocks— that God killed the herds of the Egyptians' livestock but saved the livestock of the Israelites. Then the God who created each grain of flax and barley and each human hand that planted it rained down hail on the Egyptians' crops and the men and women in the fields.

Still empire puffed itself up and would not yield. So the God who gave edible plants to humanity commanded locusts to come and eat that which the hail did not touch. And still the heart of empire was hard. And the God who separated darkness and light with the sound of his voice, that God blanketed the land of Egypt in darkness for three days. It was "a darkness that can be felt" (Exodus 10:21). And when Pharaoh's pride still would not let God's people go, God enacted the last plague "so that you may know that the LORD makes a distinction between Egypt and Israel" (11:7).

Egypt's imperial impulse to consume people and people groups for its own gain told a spiritual lie to the Egyptian people, to the Israelites, and to the world. The lie was simple: the Israelites are Egyptians because they belong to the state of Egypt. The state declared it; therefore, it was so. But the God who imprinted every human being with God's image said, "No! The Israelites belong to me. It is my image imprinted on their souls. It is I who created each ethnic group, including yours, and each person within them in my image. I am Creator God. You are not. And so that you and every other human empire may know that I am Creator, I will break your empire at its knees. The firstborn—the heirs of your empire—will be struck down at midnight." When the firstborn of every family died, Pharaoh begged God's people to go.

THE POLICIES OF GODLY GOVERNANCE

While still in the wilderness, with Pharaoh's army buried at the bottom of the Red Sea, God drafted Israel's first public policy. The first way in which the Israelites would be a blessing to all the families of the earth would be through the Ten Commandments, the cornerstone of Israel's domestic policy. Most of the commandments are written in the negative form: "You shall have no other Gods before me" (Exodus 20:3), "You shall not murder" (verse 13), "You shall not steal" (verse 15). They don't spell out rights, but the concept of rights is a modern construct. Still, we can infer that a commandment prohibiting murder conveys that citizens have the right not to be murdered. In the same way, citizens have the implied right not to be stolen from and the implied right to Sabbath.

The Sabbath in particular is a great equalizing force of the Ten Commandments. Everyone had the commandment and thus the implicit right to rest on the seventh day. The law was explicit about who "everyone" meant: men and women, slaves, immigrants in their towns, and even livestock. The Sabbath day levels the hierarchy of human value at least one day per week. On God's day, the woman, the slave, the impoverished, and the immigrant will have the image of God in them affirmed, cultivated, protected, and served. And the creatures of the earth will be able to rest and have the divine breath of life restored (see Genesis 1:30).

In the statutes God handed down to Moses a few chapters later (see Exodus 23:10–11; Leviticus 25:1–7; Deuteronomy 15:1–18), God multiplied this divine intervention every seven years by virtue of the sabbatical year. For the entire year, all of Israel is commanded to rest. In that year, all debt must be forgiven and slaves who have worked for six years must be set free. Fields must not be worked so that the poor and immigrants will be able to eat. Consider the impact of such a policy on the profitability of Israel's businesses. The sabbatical year would greatly hamper Israel's ability to build an economy that would fuel a dominating empire. If all debts were forgiven every seven years and free labor was set free, the economy would be forced to recalibrate. Here we see God placing boundaries on the world's capacity to build empire, similar to what God did at the Tower of Babel.

Sabbath and Jubilee

In Leviticus 25:8–55, God upped the ante. Every seven years, the people observe the sabbatical year, and every fifty years would be known as the year of jubilee. In the fiftieth year, not only does everyone rest regardless of their stature in the social hierarchy and not only are all debts forgiven and slaves set free, but all land goes back to the original family God gave the land to when the Israelites entered Canaan. With this policy, poverty would not be able to crush the image of God in families forever. There always would be a reset button; just hold on until the year of jubilee.

Though I do not advocate the establishment of a theocratic government, we can glean useful principles from God's system of governance:

- Regardless of one's stature within a social hierarchy, the inherent dignity of all humanity and the rest of creation should be protected, served, and cultivated by public policy.
- Godly governance places boundaries on the amount of power and influence that businesses are able to exert. Businesses are not allowed to grow to the point where they have capacity to counter God's purposes, especially in regard to the flourishing of the image of God on earth.

- Regulation is not a bad thing. It is the way governments (in a democracy, the people) place limits on the amount of injury to the image of God they are willing to allow while also accommodating economic health.[6]

In short, through the Sabbath, the sabbatical year, and the year of jubilee, as well as through a host of other regulatory measures such as gleaning laws (see Leviticus 19:9; 23:22) and other rituals, God instituted public policy to ensure protection of the ones Nicholas Wolterstorff has called the "quartet of the vulnerable"—orphans, widows, immigrants, and the poor. Wolterstorff noted in his book *Justice: Rights and Wrongs,* "In Deuteronomy 24:17 Moses enjoins the people, 'You shall not deprive a resident alien or an orphan of justice; you shall not take a widow's garment in pledge' (cf. Exodus 22:21–22). In Deuteronomy 27:19 the priests call out, in a ritualized cursing ceremony, 'Cursed be anyone who deprives the alien, the orphan, and the widow of justice,' to which the people say 'Amen.'"[7]

God wanted Israel to serve as a beacon to surrounding nations with laws that demonstrated justice. We don't know if Israel ever enacted the year of jubilee. We do know through the witness of Samuel, David, Solomon, Nehemiah, and the prophets that Israel rebelled against God's leadership and eventually turned away from God.

In the days of the priest Samuel, the Hebrews demanded their own earthly king. Like the people of Shinar at the Tower of Babel, they yearned to make a name for themselves. They wanted to compete on an equal earthly footing with surrounding nations and empires. God warned the people, through Samuel, that a king would bring war, enslavement of family members, exploitation of crops, and seizure of their land, slaves, and livestock. But Israel chose its own Tree of the Knowledge of Good and Evil. It demanded a king and got one.

King Saul brought it all. King David brought the same, plus the rape and murder of his subjects, and King Solomon added the exploited labor of thirty thousand slaves to build a Temple that God didn't want (see 1 Kings 5:13–18; 2 Samuel 7:4–7). Some scholars point to Solomon's practice of forced labor as the catalyst for the division of Israel into northern and southern kingdoms.[8]

Even under threat of destruction, God sent voices speaking shalom. Isaiah, Amos, Micah, and Hosea warned Israel and Judah about the cost of their wickedness. The prophets warned Israel and Judah of God's judgment and the destruction of both kingdoms. And in the midst of their words of judgment, the prophets also cast a defining vision of international peace and what shalom would require.

Micah penned his explicit warning to both kingdoms only thirteen years before the Assyrian Empire conquered Samaria (the northern kingdom) and 148 years before the Babylonian siege of Jerusalem, which was part of Judah, the southern kingdom. In his prophecy, Micah echoed and expanded on a vision cast by Isaiah only a few years earlier.[9]

Micah noted that the people of Israel had turned their backs on God. "They covet fields, and seize them; houses, and take them away; they oppress householder and house, people and their inheritance. . . . You rise up against my people as an enemy; you strip the robe from the peaceful, from those who pass by trustingly with no thought of war. The women of my people you drive out from their pleasant houses; from their young children you take away my glory forever" (2:2, 8–9). He pointed out that the rulers and false prophets of both kingdoms were worshiping Baal. "Listen, you heads of Jacob and rulers of the house of Israel! Should you not know justice?—you who hate the good and love the evil, who tear the skin off my people, and the flesh off their bones; who eat the flesh of my people, flay their skin off them, break their bones in pieces, and chop them up like meat in a kettle, like flesh in a caldron. . . . Thus says the Lord concerning the prophets who lead my people astray, who cry 'Peace' ['Shalom'] when they have something to eat, but declare war against those who put nothing into their mouths" (3:1–3, 5).

Micah painted a picture of the temple of Baal on Mount Ṣapān surrounded by the people of Samaria and Judah. In his description, the leaders were sacrificing their own subjects, people made in the image of Yahweh, in ritual sacrifices to Baal. Rulers were twisting the law to steal land from the people. Creditors were impoverishing men, women, and children by stripping them of their homes and even the clothes off their backs. Finally, the rulers would declare war on neighboring nations when their states' interests weren't being served and would declare peace when they were, with no concern for the suffering of the surrounding nations.

In return for their injustice, Micah declared, Jerusalem will be razed. In its place, Yahweh's house will be established on the highest mountain— higher than Baal's Mount Ṣapān. People from many nations will stream to God's house. And in the same way that the Israelites are focusing on Baal, the nations, tribes, and people groups will stream to Yahweh to learn God's way to peace. And God will govern all nations. Because God will be there in the middle of the nations, protecting them, serving them, and cultivating the image of God in all people groups, there will be no need for war. The nations will beat their swords into plowshares and their spears into pruning hooks. Instruments of death will become instruments that give life. The people will learn war no more. And everyone will have their own home with their own good land—good enough to plant vines and fig trees (see Micah 4:1–5).

During the Balkan Pilgrimage for Reconciliation, we studied Micah 4:1–5. This was prior to traveling to Dachau and before we visited Croatia, where twenty thousand people died between 1991 and 1995. Croatia was the second state to declare its independence from the former Yugoslavia after the breakup of the Soviet Union in 1989.

We studied Micah 4 before talking with a Serb veteran of the Croatian war who said the work of his life was now to regain his humanity. (The state-aligned Orthodox Church in Serbia had blessed the bombs that were dropped on Croatia and Bosnia, but a small, prophetic minority of priests resisted.) We hadn't yet traveled through the winding terrain of eastern Bosnia to Srebrenica, the small mountain town where more than eight thousand Muslim men and boys were killed in one day by Serbian troops. We would see the gravestones of Croats, Bosnians, and Serbs, all images of God obliterated across the face of Bosnia.

One young pilgrim-to-be was silent for a long time while other aspiring pilgrims shared their thoughts. Then he spoke. "The text says they gave up all of their weapons. And they didn't even *learn* war anymore." He stumbled to get his next thought out: "I mean, in order to learn basic history in grade school, we learn by memorizing which war happened when. How would we learn history if we never learned war anymore? To do that, you really can't have any fear."

With God at the center, there is no fear,

God is the source of the world's peace.

because God is the judge between nations. We don't usually think of God judging whole nations. But according to the text, God does. And the effect of God's rebuke is shalom, rest, the cultivation of life and abundance, and no fear. God is the source of the world's peace.

Years after the two kingdoms fell, the exiled priests returned to Jerusalem and penned Genesis 1, a reflection on the supremacy of Creator God, the intrinsic dignity of humanity, and the call of all humanity to exercise dominion.

Hundreds of years later, the angel of the Lord came to the virgin, Mary, and told her, "Do not be afraid." (Luke 1:30). The angel explained that the Holy Spirit would come upon Mary and she would give birth to a boy who she would name Jesus. "He will be great, and will be called the Son of the Most High, and the Lord God will give to him the throne of his ancestor David" (verse 32). A kingdom is coming.

God has broken into the universe to disrupt the reign of humanity. A confrontation is brewing between the dominion of humanity and the dominion of God. God will confront the rulers of this world in the person of Jesus.

Born in a feeding trough, honored by shepherds and international dignitaries, hunted by Herod, asylum seeker in Egypt, tempted in the wilderness for forty days and nights, Jesus stood before the people in a synagogue. They handed him the scroll. He turned to Isaiah 61 and read, "The Spirit of the Lord is upon me, because he has anointed me to bring good news to the poor. He has sent me to proclaim release to the captives and recovery of sight to the blind, to let the oppressed go free, to proclaim the year of the Lord's favor" (Luke 4:18–19). Then Jesus said to the people, "Today this scripture has been fulfilled in your hearing" (verse 21). In other words, "I just brought good news to the poor. I just proclaimed release to the captives. I just proclaimed recovery of sight to the blind. I just demanded freedom for the oppressed." The verse Jesus turned to is a direct reference to the year of jubilee. In other words, "People, though you may never have enacted the kind of dominion I prescribed from the time I established my nation, I am establishing it right here, right now."

Throughout his ministry, Jesus confronted demonic powers that, the text tells us, knew Jesus's identity as the Son of God. He also confronted the implicit biases embedded within both Jewish and Roman power structures. He touched lepers and he held theological conversations with women. And Jesus extended his power to free others to the Gentile demoniac, the Syrophoenician woman, and the Roman centurion.

Early in Jesus's ministry, he stood on the Mount of Olives and taught his followers how to pray: "Pray then in this way: Our Father in heaven, hallowed be your name" (Matthew 6:9). We have said this prayer so many times that we have lost the meaning behind it. To our ears it is nowhere near as explosive and dangerous as it would have been to Jesus followers in the first century.

The Lord's Prayer is a prayer of subversion. Caesar claimed that *his* name was the most hallowed (highest) in the world. Jesus continued to teach the way to pray: "Your kingdom come. Your will be done, on earth as it is in heaven" (verse 10). This was a direct affront to the Roman Empire, Caesar's kingdom. Jesus was telling his followers to ask God to bring God's kingdom, not Caesar's. "Give us this day our daily bread" (verse 11). Caesar tossed bread to the crowds as a sign of his benevolence to the masses. Jesus's prayer rejected bread that came in the midst of oppression. "And forgive us our debts, as we also have forgiven our debtors" (verse 12). In an occupied territory where Jewish tax collectors and Temple officials exploited the people, this is a call for the reinstitution of God's sabbatical year and the year of jubilee. "And do not bring us to the time of trial, but rescue us from the evil one" (verse 13). Rescue us from the backlash of Rome.

And then the Kingdom of God confronted the kingdoms of men directly:

- Jesus entered Jerusalem as people lined the street and waved palm branches, crying, "Hosanna to the Son of David! Blessed is the one who comes in the name of the Lord! Hosanna in the highest heaven!" (Matthew 21:9). *Hosanna* means "Oh save!"

- Jesus confronted money-changers in the Temple's Court of the Gentiles. He said, "Is it not written, 'My house shall be called a house of prayer for all the nations'? But you have made it a den of robbers" (Mark 11:17).

- Jesus went toe-to-toe with the leaders of the Temple, and he did it inside the Temple (see Matthew 22:17–22; 23:25–36).

- In the Garden of Gethsemane, on the last night before Jesus went to the cross, Peter tried to defend Jesus when guards came to seize him. Peter drew his sword and sliced off the ear of a slave of the high priest (see Matthew 26:51). Jesus said to Peter, "Put your sword back into its place; for all who take the sword will perish by the sword" (verse 52). And according to Luke's gospel, Jesus reached down, picked up the fallen ear, and healed the slave (22:51).

Why didn't Jesus brandish the sword as any king worth his legend would do? Because Jesus looked past the hands that whipped him, past the mouths that screamed "Crucify him," past the fact that all but one of his disciples were hiding as Jesus was hoisted high on a cross, past Pilate's questions, past the priests' plotting, and past Caesar's posturing. The guards arrived to take him into custody, and Jesus saw the image of God. How could Jesus strike down the image of God?

Jesus allowed the dominion of human empire to take its best shot, and he was killed. Then he rose again and God won. God beat the power of human empire not with a sword but with the power of the Resurrection.

> How could Jesus strike down the image of God?

CURRENT ENGAGEMENT

In a pluralistic democracy, we cannot impose our conceptions of God on our neighbors through the imposition of any sacred text on domestic or foreign policy. It is, though, necessary for all people of faith to draw from our principles to help us engage the world in a way that moves our nation and world toward God's very goodness. If the construction of human empire is our goal, we will become enemies of God's purposes on earth. If the flourishing of the image of God and all the relationships in creation is our goal, then we will become partners with God, exercising dominion that is in the likeness of God. We must take seriously the ways our policies (both domestic and foreign) honor or dismiss the image of God in humanity globally.

We see this principle at work from the Tower of Babel through the call of Abram; through God's confrontation with Pharaoh; through the Sabbath, the sabbatical year, and the year of jubilee; through Micah's vision; and woven throughout the Gospels. When humans aimed to elevate themselves and control their world, they inevitably crushed the image of God in the other. But when the focus was on the flourishing of the image of God, freedom was present, abundance was present, and grace was present for all.

What would it look like if current-day empires—the United States, China, the United Kingdom, the European Union—made their primary purpose the blossoming of the image of God within their borders and beyond? How would that goal alter public policy? How would it alter the way we understand our national interests in light of other nations? What would it clarify about the principle of shalom—that we all are connected? How might shalom alter the ways we think about Iran, Mexico, China's growth, ISIS, Syria, and the burgeoning refugee crisis? How might shalom impact the trajectory of the conflict between Israel and Palestinians? And how might shalom upend current policies of governments that built their wealth on lands, treasure, and dignity stolen from indigenous peoples around the globe?

Perhaps we wouldn't need to learn war . . . anymore.

Reflection Exercise

Sit with me at the foot of the Tree of Life in Revelation 22:1–2. There is no empire here. There is no coercion. There is no poverty or inequity at the foot of this tree. There are no winners or losers. The image of God thrives here. The tree produces twelve kinds of fruit each month. And for the images of God who come to the tree war-weary and defeated, the ones who have suffered under the conquest of ungodly dominions of men, the leaves of this tree are for you. Take and be healed. This is the revelation of Jesus Christ.

Shalom and Witnessing Peace

They pushed in. People crowded one another as they tried to catch a glimpse of the pope during the president and first lady's welcoming ceremony at the White House.

Pilgrims rose early in the morning—some didn't sleep at all. They rode trains, flew in planes, hailed taxis, and walked. Then they stood in lines reminiscent of a packed day at Disneyland. But this was no theme park; this was reality. President Obama and First Lady Michelle Obama had invited more than ten thousand pilgrims to welcome Pope Francis on his first visit to the United States.

I was among the pilgrims.

Perhaps more than any other person since Saint Francis of Assisi (his namesake), this pope has embodied the values and priorities of Jesus. Watching Pope Francis, the world understands on a visceral level what it might have been like to walk the earth with Jesus—to watch him embrace a leper, defend an adulterous woman, challenge the values and priorities of the religious establishment.

As we waited for Pope Francis to arrive, I asked some of the people around me why they came. I received as many answers as there were people. Some came simply to see him. Others always come to these kinds of functions. Still others spoke of the pope's capacity to unite a broken world and to emphasize the value of the least of these.

As I watched pictures of past papal visits flash across a Jumbotron screen, my eyes drifted upward and rested on the tree branch overhead. It reminded me of Zacchaeus.

All around me people in suits schemed about how they could get a better view, and it struck me: Zacchaeus was a suit guy. He was so determined to get a glimpse of Jesus that this chief tax collector scaled a tree to get a better view. Looking at that tree on the White House grounds, I understood Zacchaeus in a new way.

What was going on in his life that drove him to join the crowd? It's so easy to villainize tax collectors in first-century Judea. They exploited their own people for personal gain by overtaxing them and skimming off the top. Whole families, communities, and cities were impoverished because of tax collectors' greed. The image of God within their jurisdictions was crushed by poverty.

We usually think of the suit people as having it all together, but on that day, Zacchaeus set aside his dignity and climbed a tree. Jesus saw his desire, called him down, and engaged him in conversation. By ministering to Zacchaeus, Jesus lifted economic oppression off the shoulders of an entire town.

In Washington, DC, ten thousand pilgrims, many in business attire, strained to get close to the pontiff. A few people were standing in front of the section I was in, blocking the view of people who had been waiting for hours. The pilgrims booed. Here we were on a spiritual pilgrimage, and people in suits booed other people in suits for acting like Zacchaeus, doing what they could to get closer to God.

When the president and the pope drove past our section—only feet from our group—a great cheer rose from the crowd. Later the president spoke of the necessity of our public policy to ensure the protection of "the least of these" among us. When the pope stepped to the microphone, the crowd hushed. He opened his mouth, but we could not hear him. He spoke more softly than President Obama, plus his accent made it difficult to make out what he was saying. Just then, the crowd in the bleacher seats roared with applause. The VIPs, the insiders, could hear fine. They were being blessed. But the masses soon began to mill about and talk. Some headed for the gate, which was locked until the event would end.

> We usually think of the suit people as having it all together, but on that day, Zacchaeus set aside his dignity and climbed a tree.

I wiped tears from my eyes. These people had stopped their lives to come hear the pope. Like Zacchaeus, they were hungry for spiritual nourishment. This was an opportunity for the masses to be ministered to, but they could not hear the one they came for. So they lost interest. In that moment, they were like sheep without a shepherd.

Is this what it's like for people outside the church? I wondered. *Do they yearn for connection with God, for guidance and hope? Do they yearn for a shepherd? Do they turn their heads toward the church only to find that those in the pews are having a smash-bang time but they have no access to the blessing?*

WITNESS

In his final moment on earth before ascending to heaven, Jesus said, "You will receive power when the Holy Spirit has come upon you; and you will be my witnesses in Jerusalem, in all Judea and Samaria, and to the ends of the earth" (Acts 1:8). What does it mean to be a witness?

Random House Webster's College Dictionary gives several definitions. The clearest are "1: to see, hear, or know by personal presence and perception 2: to be present at (an occurrence) as a formal witness, spectator, bystander, etc." In general, a witness offers evidence that a claim is true or false.

Jesus tells the disciples that from that point forward, they will be his witnesses. In other words, they will be his evidence, but evidence of what?

In the church today, the idea of a witness or witnessing often feels like a marketing scheme. Workshops tend to focus on how the church can look like, feel like, and talk like what is already familiar while mastering the technology of the world in service to "the Kingdom." It's almost as if we've set up cool, alternative universes that people can enter every Sunday morning to get the week's fix before going home until the next weekly hit.

When Jesus talked about witness, he referred to our *being* his witnesses. We are to *be* his evidence as we show the world that the Kingdom of God has come.

In *The Call to Conversion,* Jim Wallis reminds us that "conversion in the Bible is always firmly grounded in history; it is always addressed to the actual situation in which people find themselves."[1] Jesus was from Nazareth, a nothing kind of town. It was one of the many northern Galilean towns where Roman soldiers had quashed a major rebellion just four years before Jesus's birth, according to Jewish historian Josephus. A general crucified two thousand men at one time. No family in the region was untouched by the bloodshed and terror.[2]

Mark's gospel opens with Isaiah's prophecy that a messenger will appear in the wilderness proclaiming the coming of the Lord. Flash to John the Baptist in the wilderness telling people they need forgiveness for their sin—the ways in which their actions or apathy had contributed to the breaking of God's shalom. John called them to repent, to turn their backs on the human kind of peace that seeks the welfare of some through the domination and oppression of others. Be baptized, John preached, and embrace God's peace *for all*! (See also Luke 3:3–15.)

Then Jesus entered the wilderness and was baptized by John. The Spirit of God descended on Jesus like a dove, and God spoke from heaven: "You are my Son, the Beloved; with you I am well pleased" (Mark 1:11). Jesus's identity is clear: he is the Son of God, the physical embodiment of the long-awaited Kingdom of God.

When Jesus came back from being tempted in the desert, he said to the people of Galilee—the families who had lived in the grip of an occupying empire and watched their loved ones die only thirty-four years before—"The time is fulfilled, and the kingdom of God has come near; repent, and believe in the good news" (Mark 1:15).

In other words, you suffered the devastation of all the relationships in creation. You lost everything when you were driven from paradise and called to wander the earth. When you trusted Creator God and chose God's ways to shalom, you were well. When you chose your own ways to wellness, however, you experienced brokenness, and sin became domination, and domination became oppression, and oppression became terror. I know it is hard for you to believe. But God is intervening today! Repent and believe that God's kind of peace—peace for all—is possible. Choose God's ways to shalom. Follow God. That is what citizenship in the Kingdom of God requires.

While Mark's account reveals Jesus's identity, Luke's account clarifies Jesus's vocation. What will the King's rule look like? We saw in the previous chapter that Jesus's first sermon in Luke 4 was a declaration of opposition to the dominion of men. In his first sermon, Jesus's vocation is clarified. It is to lift oppression and bring good news to the poor. The vocation of Jesus is to proclaim the year of the Lord's favor, a direct reference to the year of jubilee.

As we discussed earlier, the year of jubilee was one of the pillars of God's governance of Israel. Every fifty years, all debts were to be forgiven, all slaves were to be set free, and all land was to be returned to its original deed holder. In God's economy, no family would live in poverty in perpetuity. There would always be an economic reset button. We don't know if Israel ever practiced jubilee, but we do know that Jesus proclaimed it. Jesus's interaction with the tax collector Zacchaeus led that officer of the state to enact his own form of jubilee.

In Luke 4, Jesus described his vocation. It is, therefore, also the vocation of all his followers.

What does it mean, then, to be a witness? It is not enough for followers to testify with their mouth, "Lord, Lord." We must do "the will of my Father in heaven," Jesus said in Matthew 7, in order to *be* evidence of the presence of the Kingdom. We must bring good news to the poor, proclaim release to the captives and recovery of sight to the blind. We must let the oppressed go free and proclaim the year of jubilee. This is what it takes to be evidence of the presence of God's reign on earth.

N. T. Wright, in his book *The New Testament and the People of God*, explained the impact of Jesus followers in the first-century Roman Empire: "In AD 25 there is no such thing as Christianity. . . . By AD 125 the Roman emperor has established an official policy in relation to the punishment of Christians. . . . Aristides (if we accept the earlier date) is confronting the emperor Hadrian with the news that there are four races in the world, Barbarians, Greeks, Jews, and Christians."[3]

The early church was not called "the church"; it was called the Way in reference to the Jesus way of living. Driven by the Holy Spirit into the public square (see Acts 2), the Way was multiethnic and multilingual. At Pentecost, the Holy Spirit rushed in and caused all those present to speak in languages that were not their own. Each person understood the others. As we discussed earlier, God established the confusion between languages at the Tower of Babel (see Genesis 11). At Pentecost, God brought the languages together, but not in the way we would imagine. God did not unite the world under one imperial language. Rather, the power of God made it possible to have unity in the midst of diversity. God made it possible for people to speak languages that were not their own and to understand one another.

And in the same way Jesus had broken gender and class barriers, this multiethnic, multilingual group turned its back on misogyny and economic favoritism. Peter explained to the crowd why women and slaves were prophesying along with free men:

In the last days it will be, God declares,
that I will pour out my Spirit upon all flesh,
and *your sons and your daughters* shall prophesy,
and your young men shall see visions,

and your old men shall dream dreams.
Even upon my *slaves, both men and women,*
    in those days will pour out my Spirit;
    and they shall prophesy. (Acts 2:17–18)

In *The Recovery of Mission: Beyond the Pluralist Paradigm,* Vinoth Ramachandra wrote, "The Christians behaved as a new social grouping in the ancient world, a non-racial fellowship comprising both Jews and pagans. . . . The gospel constituted a new category of human being, a new way of being human. Their primary identity was found in a new familial community whose social inclusiveness was unparalleled."[4] In other words, all the cultural, economic, and gender barriers between them were broken down.

According to Ramachandra, the Jesus Way led early followers of Jesus to boycott gladiatorial spectacles and other forms of violent mass entertainment. The Way exercised the same extravagant love that Jesus called for in the story of the good Samaritan. In the prevailing culture, it was common practice to place unwanted female babies in the gutter in hopes that they would die overnight of exposure. The Way searched for these infants and saved them.[5]

Further, the Way practiced radical economic redistribution, such that there were no longer any rich or poor. Acts 2 indicates that the community held all things in common. And the writer of Acts says the group spent much time together in the Temple, the seat of civil and religious life. The Temple was not the corollary of today's church. Instead, the Temple was a place of witness for the people of the Way. The Temple also was the headquarters of the religious power that had just killed Jesus. In addition, the Temple was a place filled with people from all over the world. For the people of the Way to spend time in the Temple would be the equivalent today of spending time in gathering places and public spaces such as malls, city halls, public squares, and farmers' markets. The Temple was where the world was. And at home, the people of the Way became like family to one another. They broke bread together with joy and generosity. All of this was being a witness, providing evidence of Jesus and the Kingdom.

BELIEVING ALONE IS NOT BEING A WITNESS

In modern times, followers of Jesus chose the Way as they rose up to oppose the global slave trade, which was as common during the eighteenth century and the early nineteenth century as the Internet itself is today. And even with an end to the importation of slaves into the United States, the domestic slave trade continued for decades. Charles Finney created the altar call during the Second Great Awakening, calling slaveholders to wash clean of the sin and guilt of slavery. Finney was being a witness, living and preaching as evidence of the Way of Jesus.

In the years leading up to the Civil War, many believed that Jesus was about to come again and that he would find the nation immersed in the deep sin of slavery. Revivals broke out calling on all to repent and get clean. Phoebe Palmer was called by God to preach against slavery, but women were not allowed to preach. In 1858 she penned *Promise of the Father; or, a Neglected Specialty of the Last Days.* She argued that, according to Acts 2, in the last days the Holy Spirit would be poured out on men and women and both would be given authority by the Spirit to preach. Palmer convinced Charles Finney and others that she and other women did, indeed, deserve a speaking role on the revival circuit.

She preached in partnership with Finney, whose altar call gave the guilty the opportunity to openly declare their allegiance to the Kingdom of God. On Finney's altars lay sign-up sheets for the abolitionist movement. Waves of people entered the Kingdom of God, and slave owners released the image of God from bondage in the South. Four of those freed men were my ancestors. Four brothers were set free from their master in Kentucky between 1850 and 1860.

The suffragist movement and the civil rights movement were catalyzed, fueled, and navigated by modern-day people of the Jesus Way. They enacted creative, nonviolent strategies to confront a world hellbent on maintaining broken shalom. Alice Paul, raised a devout Quaker, was jailed for her nonviolent resistance against patriarchal empire in pursuit of one thing: women's right to vote. In 1917, enforcers of empire seized Paul, leader of the National Woman's Party, and locked her behind bars. She eventually was joined by other women in the movement. Behind bars, Paul resisted empire the only way she could. She refused to eat. Eventually, the state pried her jaw open and forced raw eggs down her throat. It broke the fast, but it did not break her spirit. Paul and her company of suffragists continued to fight for three more years until ratification of the Nineteenth Amendment in August 1920. Evidence.

Fanny Lou Hamer walked the rows of cotton in the Mississippi Delta, picking and listening to her mother sing: "Oh Lord, you know just how I feel [3x] . . . Oh Lord, we sure do need you now [3x] . . ."[6] Author Charles Marsh reveals the crucible of Hamer's faith in *God's Long Summer: Stories of Faith and Civil Rights*. She had picked cotton since she was six years old alongside her mother, father, and nineteen brothers and sisters. By 1963, Hamer found herself in the eye of the storm of the Mississippi freedom movement. Having lost her job and home the previous year for attempting to register to vote, Hamer accepted an invitation to board a bus bound for Charleston, South Carolina, to attend a citizenship school. On the way home, Hamer's Continental Trailways bus stopped at a lunch counter in Winona, Mississippi. The Interstate Commerce Commission had outlawed segregated bus depots, but many southern states refused to comply. Officers beat and arrested Hamer and four other bus passengers. Hamer suffered repeated blows to her back, hands, legs, and head with her skirt pulled up to her chin. A white officer ordered two black inmates to beat her in shifts while all the officers stood in a semicircle watching her humiliation. Her body became rock hard from the blows. She suffered permanent kidney damage and could not walk or sit after the beating. She could only lie in one position. The next day, as she sat in her cell, a hum rose from someplace deep. Then the words came:[7]

Paul and Silas began to shout, let my people go.
Jail door open and they walked out, let my people go.[8]

Fannie Lou let the rising hum carry the words from her bruised core past her broken heart and out through her bloody lips. The despair and darkness shrank back. The Spirit of God hovered over Hamer's despair and cut it with light through song. Before long, the other four bloodied prisoners sat in their cells singing "Let my people go." Marsh explains that singing brought out the soul of the black struggle for freedom. "Church broke out, empowering them to 'stay on the Gospel train' until it reaches the Kingdom."[9]

Hamer became the voice of the Mississippi movement. The following summer, she addressed the Democratic National Convention in Atlantic

City. She spoke about trying to vote and the violent retaliations. She told the story of beatings in the Winona County jail. Then, tears welling up, she concluded, "Is this America?" Thousands of people with the same faith pushed and bled until the Voting Rights Act was passed one year later. Evidence.

What does it mean to *be* a witness of the presence of the Kingdom of God in today's world? When Pope Francis visited, I was reminded of the reception Jesus received when he entered Jerusalem, the seat of power in Israel.

> What does it mean to *be* a witness of the presence of the Kingdom of God in today's world?

The people of the city said, "Blessed is the king who comes in the name of the Lord! Peace [*ereine*] in heaven, and glory in the highest heaven!" (Luke 19:38). They thought this was the moment of confrontation between the empire of Rome and the kingdom of Israel. But the moment was infinitely more significant. It was the confrontation that Luke foreshadowed in chapter 1 of his gospel. It was the moment of confrontation between the kingdoms of men and the Kingdom of God.

The people gathered in Washington, DC, flocked to Pope Francis because he has exercised dominion over the Catholic Church in a way that resembles that of Jesus's exercise of dominion.

The world watched as Pope Francis washed the feet of a Muslim girl with leprosy.

The world waited for the pope's word on climate change and gasped when he called world leaders to adopt an "integral ecology" that protects the rest of creation in a way that also protects and serves the image of God on earth—especially in "the least of these."

And the world witnessed the pope's lament over the sin-filled sexual abuse of children by Catholic Church leaders. Evidence.

People in our post-Christian nation are hungry—famished—for connection with God.

"Not in Our Town"

They watched as Michael Brown lay facedown on the street for four hours in one-hundred-degree heat in Ferguson, Missouri. They watched as Ferguson police officers and Missouri state troopers treated citizens as if they were enemy combatants. They watched law enforcement officers fail to protect Americans' rights to assemble and protest. They watched as Ferguson burned. Retired men and women in a small church in Henderson, Kentucky, watched on television as the mayhem mounted, and all they could think was, *Not in our town.*

Henderson is situated in coal and farming country. Small western-Kentucky towns are linked together by winding back roads, rolling hills, and highways. Kentucky was a slaveholding state, but it never joined the Confederacy during the Civil War. Instead, the state divided its allegiance more than any state in the nation. After the war, the Ku Klux Klan was birthed in the small town of Pulaski in neighboring Tennessee. Night riders intimidated white citizens into joining their crusade for white southern dominion. Desegregation came to Kentucky in the early 1960s. According to accounts of Henderson's leaders, the town's White Citizens' Council tried to block blacks from entering white public schools. But white and black people of faith blocked their efforts and integrated the public school despite intimidation.

Flash forward. The year is 2014. In the months after the death of Michael Brown, information about the underlying causes of Ferguson's explosion trickles out. Ferguson's criminal justice system has for years exploited black residents by targeting them for traffic tickets and fines in order to subsidize the city's budget. Schools in black areas are underfunded, and several were closed days before Brown's death. Employment practices are rife with racial discrimination, and racial bias throughout the Ferguson police department comes to light. In Henderson, faith leaders watched along with the rest of the country and realized that their own city faced different challenges but had real issues of racial injustice. Henderson would be in danger of a similar explosive event if the leaders did not reckon with the town's racial and economic history and current-day divide.

For more than twenty years, the Zion United Church of Christ in Henderson had held a Peace with Justice Weekend that attracted justice seekers from across the area. Organizers realized they needed to expand the effort to include a cross section of leaders of churches, organizations, and agencies across the town. The leadership team came together and created the Not in Our Town Justice Summit, a conversation on the intersections of race, poverty, and the criminal justice system in Henderson.

I stood onstage in front of 150 town leaders, convened by the newly formed Justice Coalition of Henderson. The coalition's leaders asked me to speak on the intersecting dynamics of race and poverty and to offer possible solutions for them to consider. In a separate presentation, the group sharpened its understanding of our nation's broken criminal justice system. The final session brought local leaders together for a frank panel discussion about the nature of the problems facing Henderson and possible solutions.

As I sat in the audience listening to town leaders wrestle with the policy implications of God's call to love their neighbor, it occurred to me that this is witness. This, right here, is what it looks like for the church to be a witness—to speak prophetically to the powers about the need for governance to serve, protect, and cultivate the image of God in every corner of every town on earth. This is witness: people who follow the Jesus Way, who believe in the power of the Resurrection, who believe that the Scriptures point the way to a better world.

In my final charge to the Henderson Justice Summit participants, I challenged the diverse cross section of leaders to consider a key lesson from Ferguson. St. Louis is located in one of the most charitable regions of the country, yet it exploited and isolated those Jesus calls "the least of these." The Ferguson Commission identified the historical, structural, systemic, geographic, and social causes of entrenched poverty in pockets of the Greater St. Louis area. Henderson sees itself as an extremely charitable town, but there is a difference between charity and justice. Charity offers a hand out or a hand up to individuals caught in poverty's web. Justice examines the web and tears it down.

The Justice Coalition of Henderson includes mainline, evangelical, Pentecostal, Catholic, Muslim, Jewish, and secular community leaders. They are beginning to imagine what it could look like to govern in a way that faces, believes in, protects, serves, and cultivates the image of God in every corner of their city. And they are beginning to organize toward the realization of that vision. This is witness.

Reflection Exercise

It is time to go and do. True witness of the reality of the Kingdom of God calls us all to embrace the very good news that black lives do matter and there is a way to restore dignity and repair the damage of centuries of degradation. True witness of the Kingdom calls every believer to embrace the image of God in himself or herself and in the other.

Witness demands that men and women live according to Paul's charge in Galatians 3 to dismantle the implicit and explicit biases and structures that undergird oppression in households, workplaces, the church, and our minds. Credible witness within families requires that we reckon with the social *and* structural impacts of governance that have served and protected some families often at the expense of those on the margins. It calls us to believe that the call to honor the image of God in all people applies within families, and it applies to public policy that affects the health of all families, especially those society presses to the margins.

Credible witness requires the church to call the nations to account for the human impacts on climate change and to change course. Witness weaves reverence for and protection of the image of God in every corner of the world into public policy decisions concerning the plight of immigrants, refugees, and internally displaced peoples. And it requires the church to call for the kind of global policy that refuses to seek the wellness of self at the expense of other nations.

Now remember the relationships inside the concentric circles of our lives (see page 34).

Consider each sphere: relationship with self, with another gender, with the rest of creation, within your family, with other ethnic groups, with other nations.

Where can you *be* a witness?

Now go and do.

Shalom and Life . . .
and Death . . . and Life

Death. Just say the word and another trails on its heels—fear.

My friend Erna got word that her father had passed away suddenly. Struggling to hold herself together, she boarded a flight for Seattle. She was going to be with the people she loved, the people who loved her. They would spend the next weeks consoling one another, remembering the man who gave Erna life, and celebrating the moments they had with him and the impact he made on their lives. Other friends of ours boarded flights to be with her in Seattle. They moved into the darkness of death to grieve with her, to hold her, and to laugh with her as she recalled funny little things about her father.

But I didn't. Death turned the corner and jumped on my friend's back. And I froze. I did nothing. I sent no cards. I made no calls. I didn't visit. When Erna returned home, I made no mention of her loss. Death—the thought of it—took me down.

I remember my first encounter with death. I was six years old, sitting in the living room of my grandmother's south Philadelphia row house. Grand-mom always had the most beautiful fish swirling back and forth in a three-by-one-foot tank. I was sitting next to the tank, and I remember the television was on and CBS was buzzing in the background. It was just Grandmom and Uncle Richie and me in the house. Grandmom was in the kitchen. Uncle Richie was upstairs in his bedroom. There was a loud thump upstairs. Grandmom ran up the stairs, using the railing to balance her aging body. I heard her cry, "Richie! Oh, Richie!" My memory stops there.

My parents told me later I wasn't at Grandmom's when Uncle Richie died. But I remember it like I was there. I've come to believe I dreamed it exactly as it happened, exactly when it happened. After that day, my grand-mother's home was quieter. Grandmom moved more slowly and seemed older.

Death. It is the great unknown. It is the abyss, the ultimate chaos, the culmination of the despair and desolation that pulsed throughout "the deep" in the beginning. Death is the ultimate separation from life, from loved ones, from self, from creation, from enemies, from being. At least that is the fear that death brings on.

Handguns are a threat because we fear death. War is a threat because we fear death. Disease is a threat because it limits life and can hasten death, even if it's the death of a particular quality of life. Legends serve to help humanity face death or even avoid it. There is a myth that our finite bodies can live forever untouched, unaffected by disease, brokenness, war, or climate. Fountains of youth and holy grails alike lift us for a moment. They help us believe, if only temporarily, that hope exists for avoiding death. We want to live forever.

Modern science has done its part to feed the mass delusion. Consider the average life expectancy in 1900, when a person could expect to live forty-nine years. Today, if you are in your midthirties, you have reason to count on living to around eighty.[1] Humanity also is enjoying a better quality of life into old age, at least the people who have money are. But what of the poor? What of the ones cheated out of the resources to buy more life? They die without dignity, and their deaths come sooner.

We have discussed the two trees that appear in the second chapter of Genesis: the Tree of Life and the Tree of the Knowledge of Good and Evil. God warned humanity, "You may freely eat of every tree of the garden; but of the tree of the knowledge of good and evil you shall not eat, for in the day that you eat of it you shall die" (Genesis 2:16–17). This is the first mention of death in the Bible. Humanity ate of the tree, and death entered the world. What did death look like? Every relationship that God declared "very good" in the beginning died a kind of death; the very goodness died. The relationship between men and women spiraled and hit ground. The relationship between humanity and the rest of creation curdled; dust and thorns rose from earth as man beat life from its arid crevices.

God took an animal that God had created, and God ripped the animal in two to cover over our shame. On that day, blood dripped from the hands of God. Then the man and woman were driven out of Eden and were separated indefinitely from the Tree of Life (see Genesis 3:22–24). I can imagine their agony. Here was a place where they had experienced the fullness of life, where all created relationships were very good. Now they would have to leave it all. If I had been there, God would have had to drive me out too.

But why was God compelled to keep humanity from living forever? Why did God drive us to confront finite days and end-of-life decisions? Why does God have the cherubim and a flaming sword guard the way to the Tree of Life? The answer just above the surface brings us back to the story: God had warned humanity that death would come if they ate of the Tree of the Knowledge of Good and Evil (see Genesis 2:16–17). They ate, so death has come. In this sense, death is simply the natural consequence of separation from God. If God is the source of life, then separation from God naturally includes separation from life itself. This is the basic truth at the heart of the Fall. At its core, the break in every relationship in God's creation, including the break between humanity and life itself, is a natural consequence and reflection of our severed relationship with God.

How can we experience life without its Author? Shame, eating disorders, gender-based violence, climate change, shattered families, racism, oppression, war, and death itself all are natural consequences of humanity's small and monumental choices to reach for peace in their own way. It is one thing to consider these truths in a solely spiritual sense, to isolate humanity's broken relationship with God and separate that brokenness from all other relationships in creation. But there is another level of logic to God's choosing to drive us from the garden. According to the text, God blocked the way to the Tree of Life to protect humanity from living forever with full knowledge of good and evil. I believe that given the deteriorating state of life on earth, natural death places boundaries on the pain of a fallen world.

> Natural death places boundaries on the despair and futility of life in the context of the Fall.

In the same way that the land placed boundaries on the chaos and despair of the deep (see Genesis 1), natural death places boundaries on the despair and futility of life in the context of the Fall. Could it be that in Genesis 3:22–24, God ushered natural death into the world as grace to humanity in a fallen world?

GREETING DEATH WITH A DANCE

In 2013, Dr. Richard Leo Twiss, a Lakota and cofounder and president of Wiconi International, died. Three days before his death, I received word that Richard had collapsed from a massive heart attack. I didn't know what to do. I felt the same pang of fear that I felt when confronted with the death of my friend's father, but this time I went to the hospital. Richard was my friend. Rather than allowing fear to guide me, I followed God's spirit of love. If I ever were to collapse in a city far from home, I would want my friends in that city to come and be with me. So I went to the hospital and found several friends holding vigil in the waiting room.

Richard's family arrived and we prayed together throughout the day. That night we learned that Richard had suffered a heart attack, heart failure, lung failure, and brain injury. According to the doctors, we would know within the next seventy-two hours whether his body would be able to heal.

The following morning, while riding the metro, I got a vision. I was anointing Richard's feet with oil. I held the vision in my heart and waited for clarification. That afternoon I received an e-mail and a phone call from the editor of the book Richard had been working on, *Rescuing Theology from the Cowboys: An Emerging Indigenous Expression of the Jesus Way in North America.* As we finished our conversation, she shared that she had a vision of someone anointing Richard's feet with oil. I shared the vision I'd had earlier in the day.

On the way to the hospital, I read the story of Lazarus and the grave (see John 11:1–44) and felt called to read it over Richard. When I arrived, I learned that during the day, Richard's kidneys had failed. I shared the two visions—mine and my friend's—with Katherine, Richard's wife and cofounder of Wiconi. She gave me permission to read the passage over Richard and to anoint his feet. As I read, we all wept. I never noticed this before, but the passage begins with an explanation that Lazarus was the brother of Mary, the woman who anointed Jesus's feet for burial. I anointed Richard's feet and prayed.

In the prayer, it was clear we were being called to believe that God was going to do a miracle. It was one of two kinds of miracles. Either God was going to say, "Richard, come forth!" and call him out of the grave. Or God was going to say, "Unbind him" from this broken body, "Let him go" (John 11:44), "It is finished" (John 19:30), "Well done, good and faithful servant" (Matthew 25:23, NKJV), thus completing the miracle that was Richard Twiss's life. As we stood around his bed, we didn't know which miracle it would be.

When I arrived back at the hospital the next morning, I sensed a sweet spirit of peace that could be explained only by the presence of the Holy Spirit. The boys played their father's favorite music. They held his hands. They joked and prayed and waited. A wonderful couple from a local church came to pray over Richard. They are native Washingtonians (Asian Americans who were born and raised here).

As doctors explained the procedure for turning off the machines, there was a strong sense in the room that God was preparing us to let Richard go. After some time, Katherine came into the waiting room where we were huddled. She said Richard had passed away. We all wept and held each other.

When we re-entered the hospital room, we gathered around our brother, father, husband, and friend. Terry LeBlanc, director of the North American Institute for Indigenous Theological Studies, officiated a traditional cedar ceremony. The boys took sprigs of cedar, crushed them, and laid them over Richard's hands, feet, and chest. Terry prayed that the smell of cedar would stay with Richard as he walked in the new place, reminding him of the land he walked on in this life. Terry sang and prayed in his native Mi'kmaq language and read Psalm 27, a favorite psalm of Richard's.

After some time, we said our private good-byes and then joined hands and did a round dance around Richard. It was beautiful. We stayed together throughout the day, toasting Richard and telling funny stories over great wine back at the hotel. Then we went out to dinner and laughed some more, telling jokes and stories.

It was at once devastating and sweet.

I can't help but think back to the moment when I anointed Richard's feet. It is clear now. We were anointing our brother's feet for burial. As I moved the oil over his feet, I repeated the words that Richard's editor had said to me when we talked earlier that night: "Beautiful are the feet of the one who brings good news."

WHERE O DEATH IS YOUR STING?

"If any want to become my followers, let them deny themselves and take up their cross and follow me. For those who want to save their life will lose it, and those who lose their life for my sake, and for the sake of the gospel, will save it" (Mark 8:34–35).

Mary Magdalene, Mary the mother of Jesus, and the other women faced down death at the crucifixion. They followed Jesus as he carried the cross up the Via Dolorosa. They walked death's road with Jesus all the way to the foot of the cross. There they watched him die. Jesus had warned his disciples that following him would mean following him to the cross, yet only the women (and John) were with him in death.

And on the third day, the women rose early to honor Jesus in death. They feared nothing; they pressed into death. They honored no one but Jesus—not the guards, not the Sanhedrin. No one. They could see only their love for Jesus.

As they approached the grave, they could see that the stone had been rolled away. The grave was open. There had been rumors that someone might steal the body, but the soldiers were still stationed right there. Jesus's body could not have been stolen. The women pushed forward to look inside.

What lives inside the grave? The grave is the storehouse for ultimate separation. The ones who have fallen prey to it live there. But not this time, not this grave. The women had the honor of becoming witnesses to the empty grave because they did not let the fear of death rule them. They witnessed glory because they were willing to walk the road to death.

As I reflect on my friend Richard, I am reminded of my paralysis in the face of death when my friend Erna lost her father. I'm not sure what made the difference this time, except that the guilt of my betrayal of my friendship with Erna haunted me for years. I had prayed for God to free me from that fear so I could be a better friend the next time.

Erna and I reconnected a few months after Richard's death. I wept as I asked for her forgiveness for abandoning her in her darkest days. I said, "I understand now . . . I understand."

She forgave me.

"Therefore, since we are surrounded by so great a cloud of witnesses, let us also lay aside every weight and the sin that clings so closely" (Hebrews 12:1). I see something in this passage now that I didn't see before I understood the very good gospel. I used to read the word *sin* and think of all my shortcomings. I would read this verse and focus on my imperfections. And I would get frustrated because I can't do things right. I will always fall short of perfection. I may as well go tank up on chocolate-glazed doughnuts now. Why even bother?

But that's not what it means. In Hebrew culture, sin had more to do with the break between relationships than with individual imperfection. It was about love and the lack of it. Original hearers likely understood the text as "Let us also lay aside every weight and the separation that clings so closely."

Separation does cling close. I experience the shadows of death in the separation within my family and in my battle to remain connected to my body, to pay attention to its needs for exercise, sleep, and healthy food. And having survived childhood sexual abuse, I experience separation in my relationships with men. These are the places where I feel the Genesis 3 Fall— the break, the wreckage—in my life. They are my Trees of the Knowledge of Good and Evil.

The constant struggle of life is to choose life, to choose God's path to very goodness rather than our own.

The call of Hebrews 12 is to lay aside the burden brought by the choices that lead to separation and death and to run be- cause we have a race to run. "And let us run with perseverance the race that is set before us" (verse 1). The Greek word translated as "perseverance" means "cheerful endurance" or "patience." I imag-

> The constant struggle of life is to choose life.

ine a person running or walking with determination, focused only on the road ahead, with a smile on her face and peace in her eyes.

"Looking to Jesus the pioneer and perfecter of our faith" (verse 2). When we feel lost and don't know which way to turn, when we encounter one of

our Trees of the Knowledge of Good and Evil, we must look to Jesus. He is our Creator. He is the author of shalom. He can show us the way to life.

"Who for the sake of the joy that was set before him endured the cross, disregarding its shame" (verse 2). Halfway through the Balkan pilgrimage, our group stopped on the Croatian island of Pag to receive several days of shalom training. One of our trainers stood in front of the group and said something I'll never forget: "To ask for forgiveness is to die a small death." Yes. And I suppose humility is a small death too, the death of supremacy. Trust is a small death, the death of control. Truth is a small death, the death of lack of accountability. Reparation is a small death, the death of domination. Reciprocity is a small death, the death of autonomy. To embrace "the other" is a small death, the death of self-absorption. But think about the alternative—choosing supremacy, control, lack of accountability, domination, autonomy, self-absorption? This path feels familiar, the path of this world. Do not be fooled; it leads to the big death and separation.

"And [Jesus] has taken his seat at the right hand of the throne of God" (verse 2). The path of the Cross, and the small deaths of repentance, humility, truth, reparation, trust, reciprocity, and embracing "the other," lead to life and resurrection. And in the light of resurrection, the big death has no sting. Separation does not win.

This gives me hope.

 Reflection Exercise

1. Reflect on "the separation that clings so closely" in your life.
2. Next do something that might feel odd at first: As you think of the separation, smile. Hold the smile for one full minute. In the middle of the smile, say to yourself silently, *Separation does not win.*

3. Consider your top one or two relationships that are suffering the pain of separation. Write them down.

4. Imagine putting aside the burden of separation. In other words, imagine choosing the way of life, love, and connection. What could that look like? Could it look like simply blessing them in your thoughts—thinking well of them? Could it look like sending up a prayer for their well-being each time you think of them? Could it look like writing in your journal a letter that you don't send to them, sharing your heartbreak and owning your part of the story? Could it look like forgiving their emotional, relational, or economic debt to you? Could it look like waiting on God to bring peace between you? Write your reflections.

5. Ask God to give you the strength to choose a path that leads to life.

6. Go back to the concentric circles from the reflection exercise in chapter 2 (see page 34). Reflect on them. How has God worked to bring healing in your relationships since the beginning of this journey?

7. Pray and thank God.

8. Ask God to continue to walk with you on the path to peace.

Conclusion

Evidence of the presence of the Kingdom of God is thick wherever and whenever people stand on the promise of God that there is more to this world—more to this life—than what we see. There is more than the getting over, getting by, or getting mine. There is more than the brokenness, the destruction, and the despair that threaten to wash over us like the waters of the deep. There is a vision of a world where God cuts through the chaos, where God speaks and there is light. There is a vision where there is protection and where love is binding every relationship together. There is a call for humanity to exercise dominion over self and the rest of creation in a way that serves all, not just self. And there is a promise that as long as we follow God's way, there will be life, healing, and love. There will come a day when all the world stands before God in shalom, and there will be only one tree, and its leaves will heal our wounds.

The very good gospel answers the heart cry of our age. Our ransacked world is crying out for the restoration of the governance of God and the shalom it brings. As the body of Christ lives out the very good gospel in pews, in households, and in the public square, it is partnering with God to restore very good (*tov me'od*) to the world. It is exercising God's kind of dominion (*radah*) within the church. And it calls our leaders to do the same in society, to exercise the kind of dominion that cultivates the image (*tselem*) of God on earth while serving and protecting all of God's creation.

Let it be so.

There is a way back to shalom. It is the way of God, demonstrated through the person of Jesus and made possible through his death and resurrection.

This is the good news. This is the very good gospel.

ACKNOWLEDGMENTS

It takes a village to raise a book. This is especially true for an informally trained Bible theologian engaging two theological concepts at the heart of Christian faith—the gospel and shalom. I am forever indebted to the village that raised *The Very Good Gospel.*

I owe the greatest debt of gratitude to the leaders of the InterVarsity Christian Fellowship's inaugural 2003 Pilgrimage for Reconciliation: Jimmy McGee (director), Dr. Randy and Edith Woodley (guides on the Cherokee Trail of Tears), Drs. Bob and Carol Hunter (guides through the African experience in the United States), and Dr. Terry McGonigal (biblical scholar). Their input and mentoring laid the foundations for *The Very Good Gospel,* and their friendship continues to this day.

I am also grateful and humbled by the enormous influence of Rev. Jim Wallis on my life and ministry. Before I knew him, he was planting seeds of understanding through his writing in *Sojourners* magazine and through his many books. For decades Jim has watered the garden of the vision of shalom through advocacy and public witness and has, in recent years, cultivated the vision in me and encourage me to speak it and write it down.

I also stand in awe of my broader Sojourners community, which understands it is not enough to write the vision: people must read it. Thanks to Charissa Laisy, whose research skills helped me write the first intimidating words on blank pages. Elaina Ramsey and Rose Marie Berger reviewed early drafts of chapters and offered excellent feedback. Rob Wilson Black,

Jim Rice, Lisa Daughtry-Weiss, Larisa Friesen Hall, Ed Spivey, Julie Polter, Sandra Sims, Betsy Shirley, Sandi Villarreal, Michael Mershon, Cynthia Martens, Simon Oh, Leticia Trujillo, and the entire Sojourners team offered feedback and skill to help as many people as possible read the vision of *The Very Good Gospel.*

Since 2014, Sojourners has convened a summit of leaders of various justice movements. For the first two years, leaders of movements for racial justice in the United States gathered on monthly conference calls to learn and deliberate together. One call early in 2014 stands out as particularly impactful. In the middle of a lively conversation between Dr. Gail Christopher, Rev. Dr. Jin Kim, Dr. Andrea Smith, Rev. Dr. Carroll Baltimore, Rev. Dr. Susan Smith, and myself, the group had a revelation: the theological antidote to racial implicit bias is the doctrine of the image of God! Yes! Thank you, village!

Some in the village introduced me to key concepts that informed portions of this text. I am grateful for the work of Dr. Miroslav Volf, who introduced me to the concepts of thin and thick faith; Mark Charles, who introduced me to the Doctrine of Discovery; and Jon Ball, who introduced me to the profound meaning of *ezer* in Genesis 2.

Likewise, networks and coalitions work out the concepts in real time. I am profoundly grateful for Christian Churches Together in the USA, Christian Community Development Association, the Samuel DeWitt Proctor Conference community, Ferguson movement leaders, Faith for Justice STL, Evangelicals for Justice, Evangelicals for Peace, NAIITS, Latino Leadership Circle, Evangelical Immigration Table, Fast for Families, the Voices Project, Red Letter Christians, Auburn Senior Fellows, Circle of Protection, New York Interfaith Coalition for Immigration Reform, Conversations for Change, and Faith Leaders for Environmental Justice. Our work together and their words around many tables helped shape the vision of *The Very Good Gospel* in my life.

There are those in the village who cultivate young leaders. They turn over soil, take up weeds, and plant seeds that grow. Their early investments make it possible for young leaders to develop eyes that see the vision in the first place. I am grateful for the Los Angeles First Church of the Nazarene and Bresee Institute led by Dr. Ron Benefiel and Michael Mata, respectively. They laid the foundations for the biblical values for racial and economic justice and multiethnic community in my life. InterVarsity Christian Fellowship in Los Angeles demonstrated the healing and reconciling power of scripture and prayer. New York Faith and Justice believed in the vision of shalom and worked with me toward its realization. And Metro Hope Church translated the vision into everyday life in the heart of Harlem!

And there are those friends who simply believe in and walk with you no matter what. Dr. Orlando and Maritza Crespo offered moral support when blank pages built mental roadblocks, while Margot Starbuck and David Zimmerman offered invaluable feedback from the book proposal to the final drafts. Thank you, village!

Finally, I am grateful for my mother, Sharon L. Lawrence, whose writing inspires and pushes me to reach for beauty and excellence, and whose life, words, and presence continue to teach and guide me. And for my family who carved space in my soul for God's shalom to pour in.

NOTES

Chapter 1: The Very Good Gospel

1. "All God's Chillun Got Wings," Negrospirituals.com, www.negro spirituals.com/songs/all_god_s_chillun_got_wings.htm.

2. See Brian Hicks, "The Cherokees vs. Andrew Jackson," *Smithsonian*, March 2011, www.smithsonianmag.com/history/the-cherokees-vs -andrew-jackson-277394/?no-ist.

3. Hicks, "The Cherokees vs. Andrew Jackson"; see also "Africans in America, Part 4: Judgment Day, Indian Removal, 1814–1858," PBS, www.PBS.org/wgbh/aia/part4/4p2959.html, and "The Supreme Court: The First Hundred Years, Landmark Cases," PBS, www.pbs .org/wnet/supremecourt/antebellum/landmark_cherokee.html.

4. "Africans in America, Part 4"; *Cherokee Nation v. State of Georgia*, 30 U.S. 1 (1831), https://supreme.justia.com/cases/federal /us/30/1/case.html.

5. For more on this, see Carl N. Lester, "A Brief History of the United States Branch Mint at Dahlonega, Georgia," Dahlonega Gold, www .dahlonegagold.com/dghist.htm.

6. David William Bebbington, *Evangelicalism in Modern Britain: A History from the 1730s to the 1980s* (London: Unwin Hyman, 1989), 2–19.

7. Gary Dorrien, *Social Ethics in the Making: Interpreting an American Tradition* (Oxford: Wiley, 2011), 87.

8. Walter Rauschenbusch, *Christianity and the Social Crisis* (New York: Macmillan, 1913), 246.

9. See Susan Curtis, *A Consuming Faith: The Social Gospel and Modern American Culture* (Baltimore: Johns Hopkins University Press, 1991).

10. Miroslav Volf, *A Public Faith: How Followers of Christ Should Serve the Common Good* (Grand Rapids, MI: Brazos, 2011), 40.

11. I owe a debt to biblical scholar Terry McGonigal, director of church engagement for the Whitworth College Ekklesia Project. It was Dr. McGonigal who taught a group of ministry staff participants on the Pilgrimage for Reconciliation—a journey that I was part of—the meanings and biblical uses of shalom. The following breakdown of the biblical use of the word *shalom* is shared from his 2003 shalom course notes and a 2016 e-mail conversation with him.

12. Walter Brueggemann, *Peace,* Understanding Biblical Themes Series (St. Louis: Chalice, 2001), 15.

Chapter 2: A Glimpse of Shalom

1. For more on this, see Gerhard von Rad, *Genesis: A Commentary,* trans. John H. Marks, rev. ed. (London: SCM, 1972), 25, 27–28; Alexander Heidel, *The Babylonian Genesis: The Story of Creation,* 2nd ed. (Chicago: University of Chicago Press, 1951), 153.

2. For more on this, see Patrick Boehler and Sergio Peçanha, "The Global Refugee Crisis, Region by Region," *New York Times,* August 26, 2015, www.nytimes.com/interactive/2015/06/09/world/migrants -global-refugee-crisis-mediterranean-ukraine-syria-rohingya-malaysia -iraq.html?_r=1.

3. For more on this, see Ashley Fantz and Ben Brumfield, "More than half the nation's governors say Syrian refugees not welcome," CNN, November 19, 2015, www.cnn.com/2015/11/16/world/paris-attacks -syrian-refugees-backlash; and Rukmini Callimachi, "Islamic State Says 'Soldiers of Caliphate' Attacked in San Bernardino," *New York Times,* December 5, 2015, www.nytimes.com/2015/12/06/world /middleeast/islamic-state-san-bernardino-massacre.html?_r=0.

4. See the *Washington Post's* ongoing report, "203 People Shot Dead by Police This Year," 2015, www.washingtonpost.com/graphics /national/police-shootings.

5. See Lenny Bernstein and Joel Achenbach, "A group of middle-aged whites in the U.S. is dying at a startling rate," *Washington Post,* November 2, 2015, www.washingtonpost.com/national/health -science/a-group-of-middle-aged-american-whites-is-dying-at-a -startling-rate/2015/11/02/47a63098-8172-11e5-8ba6-cec48b74b 2a7_story.html.

6. For more on this idea, see Yael Maschler, *Metalanguage in Interaction: Hebrew Discourse Markers* (Amsterdam: John Benjamins, 2009), 171–75. Maschler points out that while the word *tov* means "good," structurally, it is located between intonations or speakers. As in Genesis 1, *tov* marks the end of one thought and the beginning of another. It is also inherently relational; a word that occurs in the context of relationship.

Chapter 3: Two Trees and the Fall

1. For more on this idea, see Gerhard von Rad, *Genesis: A Commentary,* trans. John H. Marks, rev. ed. (London: SCM, 1972), 25, 27.

2. For more on these ideas, see Perry B. Yoder and Willard M. Swart-
   ley, eds., *The Meaning of Peace: Biblical Studies*, trans. Walter W.
   Sawatsky, 2nd ed. (Elkhart, IN: Institute of Mennonite Studies,
   2001), 1–13.

3. Walter Brueggemann, *Peace,* Understanding Biblical Themes Series
   (St. Louis: Chalice, 2001), 6–8.

Chapter 4: Shalom with God

1. For more on this idea, see Blaise Pascal, *Pensées,* trans. A. J.
   Krailsheimer, rev. ed. (New York: Penguin, 1995), 45.

2. Daniel Lynwood Smith, *Into the World of the New Testament:
   Greco-Roman and Jewish Texts and Contexts* (London: Blooms-
   bury, 2015), 133.

3. See, for instance, Abraham's servant who journeyed to the town
   of Nahor in Abraham's homeland, where the servant found a wife
   for Isaac (Genesis 24:3–4, 10–51); see also Sandra L. Gravett et
   al., *An Introduction to the Hebrew Bible: A Thematic Approach*
   (Louisville: Westminster John Knox, 2008), 141.

Chapter 5: Shalom with Self: Shame and Freedom

1. Brené Brown, *Daring Greatly: How the Courage to Be Vulnerable
   Transforms the Way We Live, Love, Parent, and Lead* (New York:
   Avery, 2012), 68, 71.

2. John Bradshaw, *Healing the Shame That Binds You,* rev. ed.,
   Recovery Classics (Deerfield Beach, FL: Health Communications,
   2006), 29.

3. Brown, *Daring Greatly,* 71–72.

4. Holly VanScoy, "Shame: The Quintessential Emotion," Psych-Central, http://psychcentral.com/lib/shame-the-quintessential -emotion.

5. Brown, *Daring Greatly,* 39.

6. Brown, *Daring Greatly,* 34.

7. See the seminal book on narcissism by Alice Miller, *Prisoners of Childhood: The Drama of the Gifted Child and the Search for the True Self,* trans. Ruth Ward (New York: Basic, 1987).

8. Brown, *Daring Greatly,* 11.

9. Brown, *Daring Greatly,* 74–75.

10. For more on this, see Walter Brueggemann, *The Prophetic Imagination,* 2nd ed. (Minneapolis: Augsburg Fortress, 2001).

11. For more on this, see Mike T. Flynn and Douglas H. Gregg, *Inner Healing: A Handbook for Helping Yourself and Others* (Downers Grove, IL: InterVarsity, 2009).

Chapter 6: Shalom Between Genders

1. For another great analysis that came to similar conclusions, see Christians for Biblical Equality, "Statement on Men, Women, and Biblical Equality," CBE International, www.cbeinternational.org /content/statement-men-women-and-biblical-equality; and Phyllis Trible, "Eve and Adam: Genesis 2-3 Reread," http://academic. udayton.edu/michaelbarnes/E-Rel103/RG4-Trible.htm#N_1.

2. Trible, "Eve and Adam."

3. Louis Bien, "A Complete Timeline of the Ray Rice Assault Case," SB Nation, November 28, 2014, www.sbnation.com/nfl/2014/5/23 /5744964/ray-rice-arrest-assault-statement-apology-ravens.

4. Jennifer L. Truman and Lynn Langton, "Criminal Victimization, 2013," US Department of Justice, Office of Justice Programs, Bureau of Justice Statistics, September 2014, NCJ 247648, 2, www.bjs.gov /content/pub/pdf/cv13.pdf.

5. United Nations Department of Economic and Social Affairs, Resolution 1993/10, "Draft declaration on the elimination of violence against women," July 27, 1993, www.un.org/esa /gopher-data/esc/res/1993/e1993-10.htm.

6. Rashida Manjoo, "Report of the Special Rapporteur on violence against women, its causes and consequences," United Nations General Assembly, Human Rights Council, Seventeenth Session, May 2, 2011, 17, www.peacewomen.org/assets/file/Resources /UN/wps__reportofthespecialrapporteuronviolenceagainst womenitscausesandconsequences_un_may2011.pdf.

7. Sharon Block, *Rape and Sexual Power in Early America* (Chapel Hill: University of North Carolina Press, 2006), 4.

8. *New York Times* Editorial Board, "The Military's Sexual Assault Crisis," *New York Times,* May 7, 2013, www.nytimes.com/2013 /05/08/opinion/the-pentagons-sexual-assault-crisis.html?_r=1.

9. "America's Changing Religious Landscape," Pew Research Center, May 12, 2015, www.pewforum.org/2015/05/12/americas-changing -religious-landscape.

10. M. C. Black et al., "The National Intimate Partner and Sexual Violence Survey (NISVS): 2010 Summary Report," Atlanta: National Center for Injury Prevention and Control, Centers for Disease Control and Prevention, www.cdc.gov/violenceprevention/pdf /nisvs_report2010-a.pdf.

11. Lifeway Research, "Broken Silence: A Call for Churches to Speak Out, Protestant Pastors Survey on Sexual and Domestic Violence," Sojourners and IMA World Health, June 2014, 4.

12. Lifeway Research, "Broken Silence," 4.

13. "2014 Pornography Survey and Statistics," Proven Men Ministries, www.provenmen.org/2014pornsurvey.

14. "Sex Trafficking," Polaris, https://polarisproject.org/sex-trafficking.

15. For more on these ideas, see Carolyn Custis James, *Malestrom: Manhood Swept into the Currents of a Changing World* (Grand Rapids, MI: Zondervan, 2015), 199–200.

16. See James, *Malestrom,* 201.

Chapter 7: Shalom and Creation

1. Marc Lacey, "Across Globe, Empty Bellies Bring Rising Anger," *New York Times,* April 18, 2008, www.nytimes.com/2008/04 /18/world/americas/18food.html?pagewanted=all&_r=0.

2. Bhawan Singh and Marc J. Cohen, "Climate Change Resilience: The Case of Haiti" (Oxford: Oxfam International, 2014), 13–17, www.oxfam.org/sites/www.oxfam.org/files/file_attachments /rr-climate-change-resilience-haiti-260314-en_2.pdf; Peter J. Jacques and Jessica Racine Jacques, "Monocropping Cultures into Ruin: The Loss of Food Varieties and Cultural Diversity," *Sustainability,* November 7, 2012, www.mdpi.com/2071-1050 /4/11/2970/htm.

3. "10 Facts About Hunger in Haiti," World Food Programme, January 12, 2015, www.wfp.org/stories/10-facts-about-hunger-haiti.

4. See Lacey, "Across Globe."

5. Joel K. Bourne Jr., "Haiti Soil," *National Geographic*, September 2008, http://ngm.nationalgeographic.com/2008/09/soil/bourne-text.

6. Matt Stevens, "California drought most severe in 1,200 years, study says," *Los Angeles Times*, December 5, 2014, www.latimes.com /local/lanow/la-me-ln-california-drought-worst-20141205-story.html.

7. Chris Megerian, Matt Stevens, and Bettina Boxall, "Brown orders California's first mandatory water restrictions: 'It's a different world,'" *Los Angeles Times*, April 1, 2015, www.latimes.com/local/lanow /la-me-ln-snowpack-20150331-story.html#page=1.

8. Chris Megerian, "Drought unlikely to cause major damage to California economy, analysts say," *Los Angeles Times*, April 14, 2015, www.latimes.com/local/political/la-me-pc-drought-impact-california -budget-economy-20150414-story.html.

9. Mona Sarfaty et al., "Key Findings National Medical Association Physician Survey," National Medical Association and George Mason University Center for Climate Change Communication, June 25, 2014, 3, 13, www.nmanet.org/images/stories/climate_change_and _health_report.pdf.

10. United Nations Women Watch, "Fact Sheet: Women, Gender Equality and Climate Change," www.un.org/womenwatch/feature /climate_change/downloads/Women_and_Climate_Change _Factsheet.pdf.

11. Henry Fountain, "Researchers Link Syrian Conflict to a Drought Made Worse by Climate Change," *New York Times*, March 2, 2015, www.nytimes.com/2015/03/03/science/earth/study -links-syria-conflict-to-drought-caused-by-climate-change.html? _r=0.

12. Lydia Polgreen, "A Godsend for Darfur, or a Curse?," *New York Times,* July 22, 2007, www.nytimes.com/2007/07/22/weekin review/22polgreen.html.

13. Benjamin F. Chavis Jr. and Charles Lee, "Toxic Wastes and Race in the United States: A National Report on the Racial and Socio-Economic Characteristics of Communities with Hazardous Waste Sites," Commission for Racial Justice, United Church of Christ, 1987, http://d3n8a8pro7vhmx.cloudfront.net/unitedchurchofchrist /legacy_url/13567/toxwrace87.pdf?1418439935.

14. GB HealthWatch, "Hazardous Waste," National Institute of Health, CDC and FDA, www.gbhealthwatch.com/hazardouswaste-details .php.

15. Bob Sussman, "The U.S. Finds Its Voice on Climate Change After Two Decades of Failed Diplomacy," Brookings, November 24, 2015, www.brookings.edu/blogs/planetpolicy/posts/2015/11/24-us-voice -climate-change-after-failed-diplomacy-sussman.

16. Randy Woodley, *Shalom and the Community of Creation: An Indigenous Vision* (Grand Rapids, MI: Eerdmans, 2012), 66.

17. See New York City's PlaNYC, a sustainability and resiliency initia-tive of the New York City Mayor's Office, www.nyc.gov/html /planyc/html/home/home.shtml.

Chapter 8: Shalom for Broken Families

1. Lisa Sharon Harper, "A Miracle of Resilience: The Story of Black Families in America Is a Testament to Persistence, Determination, and Hope," *Sojourners Magazine,* July 2015, 24.

2. Harper, "Miracle of Resilience," 24.

3. Sandra L. Gravett et al., *An Introduction to the Hebrew Bible: A Thematic Approach* (Louisville: Westminster John Knox, 2008).

4. Wendy Wang and Kim Parker, "Record Share of Americans Have Never Married," Pew Research Center: Social and Demographic Trends, September 24, 2014, www.pewsocialtrends.org/2014/09/24 /record-share-of-americans-have-never-married.

5. Wang and Parker, "Record Share of Americans Have Never Married."

6. Wang and Parker, "Record Share of Americans Have Never Married"; regarding the higher education levels of black women compared to black men, see Bryce Covert, "Black Women Are Breaking Barriers but Still Not Getting Compensated for It," ThinkProgress, April 3, 2014, http://thinkprogress.org/economy/2014/04/03 /3422550/black-women-education-work.

7. "Marriage in Black America," BlackDemographics.com, http:// blackdemographics.com/households/marriage-in-black-america.

8. Tobin Grant, "Opposition to Interracial Marriage Lingers Among Evangelicals," *Christianity Today,* June 24, 2011, www.christianity today.com/gleanings/2011/june/opposition-to-interracial-marriage -lingers-among.html.

9. Jonathan Rothwell, "How the War on Drugs Damages Social Mobility," Brookings, September 30, 2014, www.brookings.edu /blogs/social-mobility-memos/posts/2014/09/30-war-on-drugs -black-social-mobility-rothwell.

10. For more on this, see Bruce Western, "The Impact of Incarceration on Wage Mobility and Inequality," *American Sociological Review 67,* August 2002, 526–46.

11. Taylor Gordon, "The Myth Is Wrong: Vast Majority of Black Women Will Get Married in Their Lifetimes," *Atlanta BlackStar*, February 7, 2015, https://atlantablackstar.com/2015/02/07 /contrary-mainstream-media-myth-black-women-fearful-never -getting-married.

12. Claire Cain Miller, "The Divorce Surge Is Over, but the Myth Lives On," *New York Times*, December 2, 2014, www.nytimes .com/2014/12/02/upshot/the-divorce-surge-is-over-but-the-myth -lives-on.html?smid=fb-nytimes&smtyp=cur&bicmp=AD&bicm lukp=WT.mc_id&bicmst=1409232722000&bicmet=1419773522 000&_r=4&abt=0002&abg=0.

Chapter 9: Shalom and Race

1. Walter Brueggemann, *Genesis:* Interpretation, A Bible Commentary for Teaching and Preaching (Louisville: Westminster John Knox, 2010), 99.

2. Brueggemann, *Genesis*, 99.

3. Erica Ho, "Where Are the Top 10 Most Segregated Cities?" *Time*, March 31, 2011, http://newsfeed.time.com/2011/03/31/where-are -the-top-10-most-segregated-cities.

4. José Humphreys, e-mail interview with author, December 23, 2015.

5. Plato, *The Republic*, trans. Benjamin Jowett (Mineola, NY: Dover, 2000), 203–229, http://classics.mit.edu/Plato/republic.9.viii.html.

6. For more on this, see Steven Newcomb, *Pagans in the Promised Land: Decoding the Doctrine of Christian Discovery* (Golden, CO: Fulcrum, 2008).

7. "Index of Questions," United States Census Bureau, www.census
.gov/history/www/through_the_decades/index_of_questions.

8. Benjamin Franklin, "America as a Land of Opportunity," Digital
History, www.digitalhistory.uh.edu/disp_textbook.cfm?smtID
=3&psid=85.

9. For more on this, see Ian Haney Lopez, *White by Law: The Legal
Construction of Race,* 10th anniv. ed. (New York: New York University Press, 2006).

10. Matthew Hudson, " 'Blindspot: Hidden Biases of Good People'
by Mahzarin R. Banaji and Anthony G. Greenwald," *Washington
Post,* February 8, 2013, www.washingtonpost.com/opinions
/blindspot-hidden-biases-of-good-people-by-mahzarin-r-banaji
-and-anthony-g-greenwald/2013/02/08/4c42d6b8-6a1b-11e2
-ada3-d86a4806d5ee_story.html.

11. See Cheryl Staats et al., "State of the Science: Implicit Bias Review
2015," Kirwan Institute for the Study of Race and Ethnicity, Ohio
State University, 9–25, 32–34, 38, http://kirwaninstitute.osu.edu
/wp-content/uploads/2015/05/2015-kirwan-implicit-bias.pdf.

12. Michael O. Emerson and Christian Smith, *Divided by Faith:
Evangelical Religion and the Problem of Race in America* (New
York: Oxford University Press, 2000), 126–7, 132.

Chapter 10: Shalom Between Nations

1. "Jasenovac," United States Holocaust Memorial Museum, Holocaust
Encyclopedia, www.ushmm.org/wlc/en/article.php?ModuleId=1000
5449.

2. "Barracks: Station 9," Dachau Concentration Camp Memorial Site,
www.kz-gedenkstaette-dachau.de/stop09.html.

3. Nahum M. Sarna, *Understanding Genesis: The World of the Bible in Light of History* (New York: Schocken Books, 1966), 102.

4. Sarna, *Understanding Genesis,* 110; Rich Valkenet, "Bible Timeline," 2010, Bible Hub, http://biblehub.com/timeline.

5. Valkenet, "Bible Timeline"; "Egypt's Golden Empire: New Kingdom," PBS, www.pbs.org/empires/egypt/newkingdom.

6. For more on this idea, see Aneel Karnani, "The Case Against Corporate Social Responsibility," *Wall Street Journal,* August 23, 2010, www.wsj.com/articles/SB1000142405274870333800457523011 2664504890; also listen to Arneel Karnani, interview with *Wall Street Journal* Online, http://podcast.mktw.net/wsj/audio/20100818/pod-wsjjrkarnani/pod-wsjjrkarnani.mp3.

7. Nicholas Wolterstorff, *Justice: Rights and Wrongs* (Princeton, NJ: Princeton University Press, 2008), 75.

8. Sandra L. Gravett et al., *An Introduction to the Hebrew Bible: A Thematic Approach* (Louisville: Westminster John Knox, 2008), 300.

9. Gravett et al., *An Introduction to the Hebrew Bible,* 32, 316; see also Valkenet, "Bible Timeline."

Chapter 11: Shalom and Witnessing Peace

1. Jim Wallis, *The Call to Conversion: Why Faith Is Always Personal but Never Private,* rev. ed. (San Francisco: HarperCollins, 2005), 6.

2. Josephus, "Antiquities 17: Book 10," in James D. Tabor, "The Jewish Roman World of Jesus," University of North Carolina at Charlotte, https://clas-pages.uncc.edu/james-tabor/archaeology-and-the-dead-sea-scrolls/josephus-references-to-crucifixion/#

3. N. T. Wright, *The New Testament and the People of God* (London: SPCK, 1992), 359.

4. Vinoth Ramachandra, *The Recovery of Mission: Beyond the Pluralistic Paradigm* (Grand Rapids, MI: Eerdmans, 1997), 226.

5. For more on this, see Ramachandra, *Recovery of Mission.*

6. Fannie Lou Hamer, "Oh Lord, You Know Just How I Feel," *Songs My Mother Taught Me,* copyright © 2015, Smithsonian Folkways Recordings.

7. See Charles Marsh, *God's Long Summer: Stories of Faith and Civil Rights* (Princeton, NJ: Princeton University Press, 1997), 10–21.

8. Fannie Lou Hamer, "Go Tell It on the Mountain, Let My People Go," *Lest We Forget, Vol. 1: Movement Soul, Sounds of the Freedom Movement in the South, 1963–1964,* copyright © 1980, Smithsonian Folkways Recordings.

9. See Marsh, *God's Long Summer,* 22.

Chapter 12: Shalom and Life . . . and Death . . . and Life

1. For more on this, see David Leonhardt, "Life Expectancy Data," *New York Times,* September 27, 2006, www.nytimes.com/2006/09/27/business/27leonhardt_sidebar.html?_r=0.